PHONICS
FOR OLDER STUDENTS

REM 800

A TEACHING RESOURCE FROM...

©2000

To find Remedia products in a store near you, visit:
http://www.rempub.com/stores

REMEDIA PUBLICATIONS, INC.
15887 N. 76TH STREET • SUITE 120 • SCOTTSDALE, AZ • 85260

INTRODUCTION

This book was designed especially for the student who has been introduced to vowel sounds but still needs further practice to reach mastery levels.

For additional phonics fun, try these high-interest phonics puzzles! They make great seatwork activities and offer lots of practice:

REM 810A *Phonics Crosswords*
REM 810B *Phonics Word Search*

CONTENTS

Pre/Post Test

Directions: Circle all words that have a short vowel sound.

bake	fade	sad	wait
clap	same	bean	hat
fad	said	clash	that
mad	made	hate	date

Directions: Circle the word that will complete each sentence. Write the word on the line.

1. That black cat may _____ you.   **mad**   **scratch**   **sack**

2. Can Dan see that _____?   **flag**   **thank**   **mad**

3. That _____ is soft and green.   **hatch**   **grass**   **ranch**

4. The big _____ fell from our tree.   **crash**   **gas**   **branch**

5. Please do not _____ the door.   **slap**   **slam**   **clam**

6. Do you think the egg will _____?   **crack**   **back**   **sand**

7. Put more milk in my _____.   **gas**   **grass**   **glass**

8. She put a _____ on his pants.   **hatch**   **pan**   **patch**

9. Did you hear the _____ play?   **lamp**   **band**   **lamb**

10. My dog likes to _____ his tail.   **wag**   **sag**   **shag**

Name _____

Short Vowel Rule:
If a word has only one vowel and it is at the beginning or between consonants, that vowel usually stands for a short sound.

Directions: Say the name of each picture. Draw a circle around its name. Write the word.

1.		ant	ax	and	_____
2.		tan	track	tag	_____
3.		plan	pan	patch	_____
4.		hand	hatch	hang	_____
5.		bank	back	bag	_____
6.		ran	rat	rang	_____
7.		mat	map	mad	_____
8.		sack	slap	sand	_____

Choose five of the words above and write a sentence for each word.

> **REMEMBER** - If a word has only one vowel and it is between consonants, that vowel usually stands for a short sound.

Directions: Circle each word that has a short A sound. Write the word.

lane	_____	paid	_____
land	_____	tap	_____
bath	_____	lap	_____
case	_____	flash	_____
crash	_____	cape	_____
tramp	_____	save	_____

Directions: Put a check (✓) by each word that has a short A sound. Write the word.

stand	_____	made	_____
said	_____	head	_____
lamp	_____	slap	_____
rate	_____	last	_____
stack	_____	grab	_____
lab	_____	bait	_____

Directions: Underline each word that has a short A sound. Write the word.

plan	_____	gas	_____
plane	_____	gave	_____
snake	_____	drag	_____
brand	_____	fact	_____
grass	_____	face	_____
lamb	_____	blast	_____

Directions: Find short A vowel words in the box. Write them on the lines.

flag	bath	rat	pat
same	bake	pan	clash
ate	stack	made	class
blame	cane	hate	date
at	hat	clap	blast
quack	crash	cap	rate
sack	cape	make	crate
fade	mad	drag	last

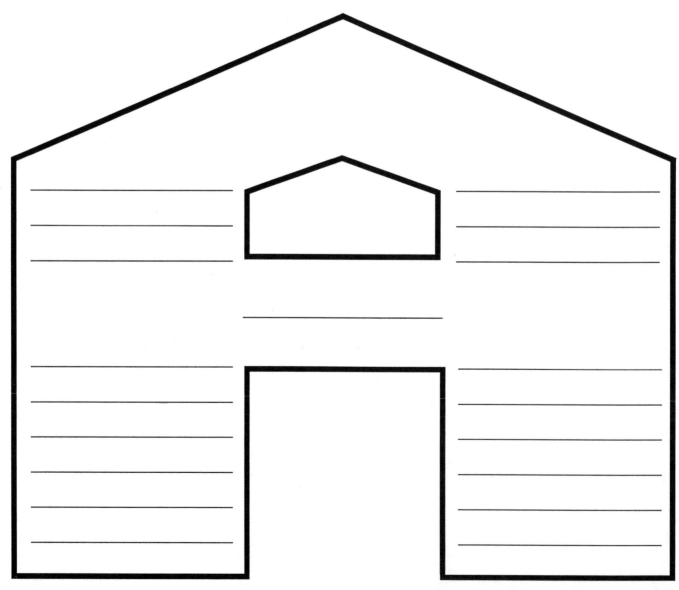

Name _____

Directions: Read each sentence. Circle each word that has a short A sound.

1. That lamp has a green shade.

2. The brass pan fell from its place on the shelf.

3. I hope you will pass the class.

4. The bat flew back into the cave.

5. I hope the black pants do not fade.

6. Did he grab the bag from the gate?

7. He said, "I will be there in a flash."

8. I will take a nap on the soft, green grass.

You should have circled 16 words. Write the circled words in alphabetical order.

1. _____   9. _____

2. _____   10. _____

3. _____   11. _____

4. _____   12. _____

5. _____   13. _____

6. _____   14. _____

7. _____   15. _____

8. _____   16. _____

Name _____

Directions: Circle the word that will complete each sentence. Write the word on the line.

1. The man's car had a _____ tire.   **flat**   **snag**   **fat**

2. Hand the bag of _____ to Sam.   **tacks**   **last**   **camp**

3. Put the brass _____ on the stand.   **had**   **lamp**   **chance**

4. The black _____ drank from the can.   **crash**   **lamp**   **lamb**

5. Stan put the cash in the big _____.   **drag**   **bag**   **brand**

6. We saw a crab on the _____.   **sand**   **clam**   **dance**

7. Ask Dan to cut the man's _____.   **drank**   **fact**   **grass**

8. Ann drove past the the big _____.   **pack**   **ranch**   **ask**

9. Use a _____ to wipe the car.   **rap**   **rag**   **ranch**

10. Jack was _____ to see his dad.   **glass**   **glad**   **grab**

11. The man _____ in the big lake.   **stand**   **strap**   **swam**

12. It was the _____ game of the year.   **last**   **lad**   **lass**

Name _____

Directions: Put each short A word from the box into its correct shape. Then write the word on the line.

stack	that	grab	back	stand
glass	am	lamb	act	grass
fast	land	pants	last	cast
cap	lamp	brand	shack	hatch

1. _____

2. _____

3. _____

4. _____

5. _____

6. _____

7. _____

8. _____

9. _____

10. _____

11. _____

12. _____

13. _____

14. _____

15. _____

16. _____

17. _____

18. _____

19. _____

20. _____

7

Directions: Add and subtract letters to find new short A words. Write the words.

1.   black - lck + th   _____

2.   patch - tch + nt   _____

3.   plank - k + t   _____

4.   clap - p + ss   _____

5.   sack - ck + nd   _____

6.   track - ck + mp   _____

7.   grass - ss + nt   _____

8.   patch - ch + h   _____

9.   rang - g + ch   _____

10. lamb - mb + ck   _____

Put the new words you have written in alphabetical order.

1.   _____   6.   _____

2.   _____   7.   _____

3.   _____   8.   _____

4.   _____   9.   _____

5.   _____   10. _____

Name _____

Directions: Each short A word is written in code. Decode each word, then write the word.

a	b	c	d	e	f	g	h	i	j	k	l	m
1	2	3	4	5	6	7	8	9	10	11	12	13
n	o	p	q	r	s	t	u	v	w	x	y	z
14	15	16	17	18	19	20	21	22	23	24	25	26

1. 7-12-1-4 _____

2. 16-1-19-20 _____

3. 2-18-1-19-19 _____

4. 3-1-13-16 _____

5. 18-1-3-11 _____

6. 3-1-20-3-8 _____

7. 1-19-11 _____

8. 7-18-1-14-20 _____

9. 7-1-19 _____

10. 7-18-1-2 _____

11. 1-14-4 _____

12. 19-12-1-16 _____

13. 12-1-3-11 _____

14. 2-1-20 _____

15. 3-1-19-20 _____

16. 3-12-1-19-19 _____

Put the words you have written in alphabetical order.

1. _____

2. _____

3. _____

4. _____

5. _____

6. _____

7. _____

8. _____

9. _____

10. _____

11. _____

12. _____

13. _____

14. _____

15. _____

16. _____

Name _____

Find the words below in the word search puzzle.

```
B A T O L S H D A N C E P Q D I D
R S A N D B A H S E E T H X N C P
B F O P H L T G A T H N K U S W L
L G R S Y A C C R A C K U V N L A
A O T O B E T N C L A S S R A P M
C I H O O L G C Q R X W P Z P E B
K T H A N K B O H L M F A S T F G
A B C D E F Q H I J K L M N O D P
T A N Q R G A S S T H A T C A U A
V D W X Y Z S O O E A X I M G H S
M A T C H T K R R M N Q P A S Z T
S A T O G T U X E F L A G O Q R T
B P G L A S S F R A N C H H S A M
```

mash	ranch	flag
hatch	past	damp
bat	sat	that
tan	bath	tag
black	than	crack
lamb	class	ask
sand	thank	ax
fast	gas	snap
match	glass	map

Name _____

Directions: Use each word group in a sentence.

cash to the bank

1. _____

my tan backpack

2. _____

a sack of sand

3. _____

big, brass lamp

4. _____

a gas can

5. _____

my black cap

6. _____

sat on the grass

7. _____

ask the man

8. _____

Name _____

Directions: Fill in each blank with a short A word that rhymes with the underlined word. Choose a word from the box.

lamp	bag	jam	last	lap
crab	sack	mad	pan	fat

1. The old <u>man</u> ran over a _____.

2. The <u>rag</u> was in a _____.

3. He was <u>fast</u>, but came in _____.

4. We ate <u>ham</u> with _____.

5. My <u>dad</u> was really _____.

6. The old black <u>cat</u> was _____.

7. There was a <u>stamp</u> on the _____.

8. Put the <u>tack</u> in the _____.

9. He put his <u>cap</u> in his _____.

10. I saw him <u>grab</u> the _____.

Write four rhyming words for each of the words below.

fan	hat	hand	back
_____	_____	_____	_____
_____	_____	_____	_____
_____	_____	_____	_____
_____	_____	_____	_____

Name _____

Directions: Find a word in each box to answer each riddle.

lamp	bath	gas	sand	crash
rack	quack	band	ax	dam

1.   I'm on the beach. What am I?   _____

2.   I give light. What am I?   _____

3.   I can chop wood. What am I?   _____

4.   I make music. What am I?   _____

5.   I can hold a book. What am I?   _____

6.   I am a loud sound. What am I?   _____

7.   I can make you clean. What am I?   _____

8.   I am the sound a duck makes. What am I?   _____

9.   I can make a car go. What am I?   _____

10. I can hold back water. What am I?   _____

Put the words in the box in alphabetical order.

1. _____   6. _____

2. _____   7. _____

3. _____   8. _____

4. _____   9. _____

5. _____   10. _____

Name _____

Directions: Find a word in the box to write on the line.

cash	black	sand	back
grass	bad	that	ask
pan	sad	catch	bat

1. Not a ball, but a _____

2. Not a check, but _____

3. Not weeds, but _____

4. Not throw, but _____

5. Not front, but _____

6. Not a pot, but a _____

7. Not this, but _____

8. Not tell, but _____

9. Not white, but _____

10. Not good, but _____

11. Not happy, but _____

12. Not dirt, but _____

Choose five words from the word box. Use each word in a sentence.

1. _____

2. _____

3. _____

4. _____

5. _____

Name _____

Step 1: Choose a word from the word box to complete each sentence.

Step 2: Complete each puzzle with the word that you have used in the sentence.

rash	sack	patch	pants	brass
snap	black	grass	tack	crack

1. My dad sat on a _____ t a c k _____.

2. His _____ were too big on him.

3. The _____ was very damp.

4. My _____ is full of rocks.

5. The baby had a bad _____.

6. There was a _____ in the glass.

7. Pat lost her big, _____ cat.

8. There was a small _____ of grass in the yard.

9. I saw the man _____ his fingers.

10. The _____ lamp was very big.

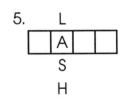

1.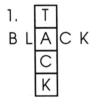

2.

3.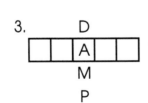

4.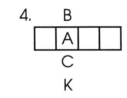

5.   L
   □□A□□
      S
      H

6.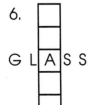

7.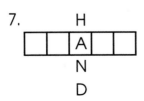

8.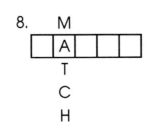

9. □
  C A M P
    □
    □

10.   L
   □□A□□
      M
      P

©Remedia Publications   15   PHONICS

Name _____

Directions: Write a synonym (a word that means almost the same) for each word. Use the words from the box.

money	ground	pot
insect	twig	break
happy	boy	sack
girl	lawn	father
bum	rest	

1. grass _____

2. branch _____

3. bag _____

4. tramp _____

5. crack _____

6. glad _____

7. nap _____

8. lad _____

9. lass _____

10. pan _____

11. dad _____

12. ant _____

13. cash _____

14. land _____

Write the short A words in alphabetical order.

1. _____

2. _____

3. _____

4. _____

5. _____

6. _____

7. _____

8. _____

9. _____

10. _____

11. _____

12. _____

13. _____

14. _____

Name _____

Directions: Write an antonym (opposite) for each word. Use words from the box.

subtract	slow	woman
front	white	walked
good	thin	tell
sea	throw	happy
first	dry	

1. fat _____

2. add _____

3. bad _____

4. last _____

5. back _____

6. fast _____

7. catch _____

8. land _____

9. damp _____

10. ask _____

11. black _____

12. ran _____

13. sad _____

14. man _____

Write the short A words in alphabetical order.

1. _____

2. _____

3. _____

4. _____

5. _____

6. _____

7. _____

8. _____

9. _____

10. _____

11. _____

12. _____

13. _____

14. _____

Name _____

Directions: Fill in each blank with a short A compound word. Use words from the box.

backpack	**hatchback**	**backhand**
handstand	**grandstand**	**hangman**
handbag	**sandman**	**crabgrass**

1. We sat in the _____ at the rodeo.

2. My dad's new car has a _____.

3. That tennis player has a great _____!

4. Did your mother lose her black _____?

5. My best friend and I played _____.

6. My little sister thinks the _____ comes each night.

7. Watch me do a _____ on the grass.

8. We have _____ growing in our yard.

9. You can put your books in my _____.

Directions: Divide the words in the box into syllables.

1. _____ / _____

2. _____ / _____

3. _____ / _____

4. _____ / _____

5. _____ / _____

6. _____ / _____

7. _____ / _____

8. _____ / _____

9. _____ / _____

Directions: Read the story. Then answer the questions.

Mack the cat is tan and black . . . and fat! He never misses a chance for a nap. In fact, he naps and snacks all day. One day, he sat up fast when he heard a scratch near his mat. He saw a rat looking back at him.

"That rat is no match for this cat," said Mack.

He got a sack and sat near the rat's path. He sat, wagging his tail, waiting to grab the rat and drag it away. The rat dashed past Mack faster than a snap.

1. What is the cat's name?

   _____

2. Why is he fat?

   _____

3. What made him sit up fast?

   _____

4. In what was he going to put the rat?

   _____

5. Did Mack catch the rat?

   _____

6. Why or why not?

   _____

Name _____

Directions: Read the story. Then answer the questions.

Sam Slabb had a yak named Sally. He planned to teach Sally how to dance. He wanted to have an act - Sam and his Dancing Yak.

Sam camped in Sally's pasture with his banjo. He sang, clapped his hands, and tapped his foot day after day. Sally just ate grass and wagged her tail. She had no plan to learn how to dance.

One day, as Sam took a nap, Sally ate his banjo. Sam packed up and stamped back to his house. Sam was very mad, but Sally the Yak was as happy as a clam.

1. Who was Sally?

    _____

2. Who was her owner?

    _____

3. What did Sam want to do?

    _____

4. What were three things he did to make Sally want to dance?

    _____

5. What did Sally do to Sam's Banjo?

    _____

6. How did Sally feel after Sam went home?

    _____

Pre/Post Test

Directions: Circle all words that have a short vowel sound.

send	sleep	shell	cheese
speed	peach	sneak	peek
neck	when	dress	sled
yell	tent	chest	west

Directions: Circle the word that will complete each sentence. Write the word on the line.

1. The red vase is on the _____.   **neck**   **west**   **chest**

2. My sister put a _____ in her car.   **end**   **dent**   **went**

3. I can _____ the rip in your shirt.   **mend**   **beg**   **lend**

4. Did he _____ all the money?   **sent**   **sped**   **spend**

5. Put the _____ on your pants.   **bet**   **belt**   **bled**

6. Do you have cash to pay the _____?   **edge**   **red**   **rent**

7. We slept in a _____ on our trip.   **tent**   **rest**   **kept**

8. The small _____ fell from the big tree.   **test**   **nest**   **neck**

9. He left this _____ on the beach.   **shed**   **shell**   **step**

10. The _____ has a nest in our tree.   **wren**   **vest**   **pet**

Short Vowel Rule:
If a word has only one vowel and it is at the beginning or between consonants, that vowel usually stands for a short sound.

Directions: Say the name of each picture. Draw a circle around its name. Write the word.

1.		bell	belt	beg	_____
2.		edge	end	egg	_____
3.		leg	led	lend	_____
4.		next	nest	neck	_____
5.		pet	peg	pen	_____
6.		shelf	shell	shed	_____
7.		net	next	nest	_____
8.		wet	went	web	_____

Choose five of the words above and write a sentence for each word.

Name _____

REMEMBER - If a word has only one vowel and it is between consonants, that vowel usually stands for a short sound.

Directions: Circle each word that has a short E sound. Write the word.

swept _____   seem _____

bean _____   rent _____

beg _____   seam _____

chest _____   pest _____

same _____   mend _____

vest _____   team _____

Directions: Put a check (✓) by each word that has a short E sound. Write the word.

fled _____   smell _____

sneeze _____   feet _____

bless _____   sled _____

west _____   sell _____

need _____   then _____

weed _____   peek _____

Directions: Underline each word that has a short E sound. Write the word.

jest _____   next _____

seat _____   greet _____

seek _____   dress _____

melt _____   when _____

yell _____   heel _____

sped _____   wed _____

Name _____

Directions: Find short E words in the box. Write them on the lines.

test	bet	steep	press
heat	kept	them	next
cheek	keep	fear	cheer
yes	wheel	breeze	lend
felt	hen	when	week
weed	bend	steel	sweep
stretch	seed	breed	chest
pet	belt	swept	egg

_____

_____   _____

_____   _____

_____

_____

_____   _____

_____   _____

_____

_____   _____

_____   _____

_____

Choose 5 of the words you have written. Write a sentence for each word.

Name _____

Directions: Circle the word that will complete each sentence. Write the word on the line.

1. We _____ in the brown tent.   **sent**   **slept**   **speck**

2. I will write a _____ to pay the bill.   **check**   **cent**   **chest**

3. I cut my hand and it _____.   **bent**   **bled**   **bed**

4. He put his book on the _____.   **self**   **shelf**   **sell**

5. She had the _____ on her desk.   **tell**   **ten**   **test**

6. Put the _____ on your plate.   **bless**   **egg**   **end**

7. Next Monday, we can pay the _____.   **rent**   **red**   **wreck**

8. Did you see the _____ crack?   **spell**   **shell**   **sell**

9. I think I can _____ my shirt.   **met**   **melt**   **mend**

10. Do not _____ too much money.   **spend**   **sped**   **swell**

Use each of the following phrases in a sentence:

     red sled   **best dress**   **ten cents**

Name _____

Directions: Put each short E word from the box into its correct shape. Then write the word on the line.

keg	wed	chest	kept	less
swept	vest	went	chess	lend
slept	fell	pen	mess	met
bed	test	desk	men	pet

1. 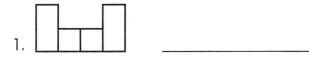 _____

2. 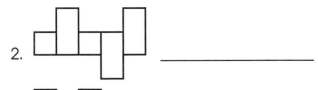 _____

3.  _____

4.  _____

5.  _____

6. 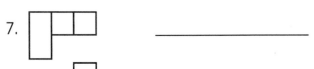 _____

7.  _____

8.  _____

9. _____

10. _____

11.  _____

12.  _____

13.  _____

14.  _____

15.  _____

16.  _____

17. _____

18. _____

19. _____

20. _____

Directions: Each short E word is written in code. Decode each word, then write the word.

a	b	c	d	e	f	g	h	i	j	k	l	m
1	2	3	4	5	6	7	8	9	10	11	12	13

n	o	p	q	r	s	t	u	v	w	x	y	z
14	15	16	17	18	19	20	21	22	23	24	25	26

1. 3-5-14-20 _____
2. 19-23-5-12-12 _____
3. 19-16-5-14-20 _____
4. 23-18-5-14 _____
5. 2-5-12-20 _____
6. 19-13-5-12-12 _____
7. 8-5-12-16 _____
8. 19-8-5-4 _____

9. 19-12-5-4 _____
10. 6-12-5-4 _____
11. 19-16-5-12-12 _____
12. 20-18-5-14-4 _____
13. 12-5-14-4 _____
14. 18-5-14-20 _____
15. 13-5-12-20 _____
16. 14-5-3-11 _____

Put the words you have written in alphabetical order.

1. _____
2. _____
3. _____
4. _____
5. _____
6. _____
7. _____
8. _____

9. _____
10. _____
11. _____
12. _____
13. _____
14. _____
15. _____
16. _____

Name _____

Find the words below in the word search puzzle.

```
V E N T L S W E S T C E P T N E C
S S A N D B O Y S E E T H A N C L
H F O P Q N E C K T N N K U S X E
E G R B Y Z T A Z E E C U V N L S
L D N E P S I N H L A D S R A X S
L I H S O L G W L R N W Y D N C L
N E X T N K B E C E M F A T E Y G
A B L E S S W H B J K S T R E S S
T A N Q R S K S S T H H T C H U E
V D W S T R E T C H L E N D G H N
M R T C H T P R R M N D T A S Z T
R E N T G T X A M N D M E L T R T
B D G L A T R E N D N C K E P T M
```

spend	best	vent
when	stress	less
bless	shed	swell
kept	west	lend
trend	shell	sent
cent	neck	next
stretch	bend	melt
red	rent	yet

Name _____

Directions: Use each word group in a sentence.

tall, red chest

1. _____

her best dress

2. _____

ten cents

3. _____

wren in the nest

4. _____

fed his pet

5. _____

Ted's new sled

6. _____

shell on the shelf

7. _____

hens in the pen

8. _____

Write these words in alphabetical order: bend   bled   fled   fed

1. _____   3. _____

2. _____   4. _____

Directions: Write a pair of rhyming words in each circle. Use words from the box.

chest	sped	spell	dent	bled	spent	swell
deck	check	when	west	dress	then	press

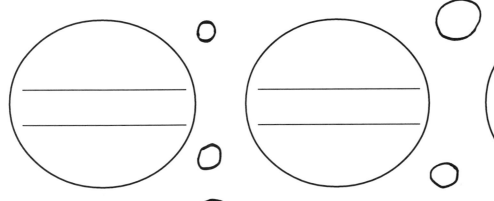

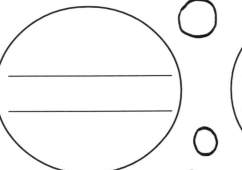

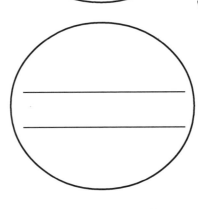

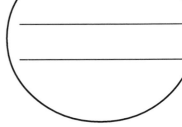

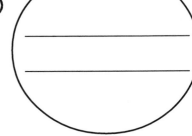

Write a rhyming word for each word below.

1. send _____

2. less _____

3. tent _____

4. hen _____

5. fed _____

6. west _____

Directions: Fill in each blank with a short E word that rhymes with the underlined word. Choose a word from the box.

pet	slept	bell	mess	chest
well	tent	test	red	pen

1. Mom put my <u>vest</u> in the _____.

2. The <u>hen</u> was in the _____.

3. My mom <u>swept</u> as I _____.

4. I am going to <u>get</u> a _____.

5. The <u>shed</u> was painted _____.

6. Meg wanted to <u>sell</u> the _____.

7. The man <u>went</u> into the _____.

8. My old <u>dress</u> was a _____.

9. He doesn't <u>spell</u> so _____.

10. She did the <u>best</u> on the _____.

Write four rhyming words for each of the words below.

bend	bell	sent	best
_____	_____	_____	_____
_____	_____	_____	_____
_____	_____	_____	_____
_____	_____	_____	_____

Name _____

Directions: Find a word in the box to answer each riddle.

belt	test	pen	bell	chest
ten	neck	shed	hen	egg

1. I have a shell. What am I? _____

2. I live on a farm. What am I? _____

3. I am a place to keep tools. What am I? _____

4. I can hold your clothes. What am I? _____

5. I can find out what you know. What am I? _____

6. I fit around your waist. What am I? _____

7. I am part of your body. What am I? _____

8. I can hold ink. What am I? _____

9. I can ring. What am I? _____

10. I am more than nine. What am I? _____

Write the words in the box in alphabetical order.

1. _____   6. _____

2. _____   7. _____

3. _____   8. _____

4. _____   9. _____

5. _____   10. _____

Name _____

Directions: Find a word in the box to write on the line.

hen	west	red	men
best	pen	them	yes
leg	bent	tenth	bed

1. Not east, but _____

2. Not a pencil, but a _____

3. Not pink, but _____

4. Not a rooster, but a _____

5. Not no, but _____

6. Not ninth, but _____

7. Not a chair, but a _____

8. Not straight, but _____

9. Not us, but _____

10. Not worst, but _____

11. Not boys, but _____

12. Not an arm, but a _____

Choose 4 words from the word box. Use each word in a sentence.

1. _____

2. _____

3. _____

4. _____

Name _____

Directions: Write a synonym (a word that means almost the same) for each word. Use words from the box.

damp	jewel	snoozed
sniff	gown	fix
iron	finish	married
exam	cried	shout
placed	cot	

1. wed _____

2. set _____

3. slept _____

4. gem _____

5. press _____

6. smell _____

7. bed _____

8. test _____

9. wept _____

10. yell _____

11. end _____

12. wet _____

13. dress _____

14. mend _____

Write a sentence for each word.

1. gem _____

_____

2. wept _____

_____

3. press _____

_____

4. wed _____

_____

Name _____

Directions: Write an antonym (opposite) for each word. Use words from the box.

more	saved	ask
came	begin	women
freeze	dry	buy
whisper	no	rooster
woke	worst	

1. wet _____

2. less _____

3. men _____

4. went _____

5. best _____

6. spent _____

7. slept _____

8. tell _____

9. sell _____

10. end _____

11. melt _____

12. yes _____

13. yell _____

14. hen _____

Write the short E words in alphabetical order.

1. _____

2. _____

3. _____

4. _____

5. _____

6. _____

7. _____

8. _____

9. _____

10. _____

11. _____

12. _____

13. _____

14. _____

Name _____

Read the story. Then answer the questions.

Betsy Bird lived in an old elm tree on the edge of the big woods. Betsy had a nice nest that she kept very neat. In her nest were three eggs. When she slept, she spread her wings over the eggs. This kept them from getting wet.

One night, a very bad storm swept through the big woods. Betsy's nest fell from the tall elm. Betsy was in a real mess. How would she get her nest and the three eggs back up in the tree? First she sat down and wept. Then she yelled for help. That didn't get her anywhere. At last she went to ask her friends, the squirrels, for help.

They set about getting the nest back up the tall elm. No sooner was this done than the eggs hatched. Betsy was kept very busy with three mouths to be fed and a messy nest to mend. But she felt very good about having friends that would lend a hand and help her when trouble came.

1. What was the bird's name? _____

2. Where did she live? _____

3. How many eggs were in the nest? _____

4. What made the nest fall? _____

5. Who helped Betsy? _____

6. What made Betsy feel good? _____

_____

BONUS: Find 20 short E words in the story. Circle them.

Name _____

Read the story. Then answer the questions.

Ben Beck wanted a sled. Every day he left school and went to Speck's Store. Speck's had the best sled Ben had ever seen. When the first snow came, Ben kept his eye on that sled. It was red, and Mr. Speck said he would sell it for ten dollars. Even when Ben slept, he saw himself on that swell, red sled.

One day he set his bank on his desk and added up every cent he had. He had only seven dollars. Where would he get the rest? Mr. Bell, who lived next door, asked Ben to help mend a hole in his fence. He paid him two dollars. Then his Uncle Ted sent him a letter and a crisp, new dollar bill. At last he had his ten dollars. He sped to Speck's store the next day to get the best red sled in the whole world.

1. What did Ben want? _____

2. Where was the sled? _____

3. What did Ben do every day after school? _____

   _____

4. How much did the sled cost? _____

5. How much money did Ben have in his bank? _____

6. Tell the two ways Ben got the rest of the money. _____

   _____

BONUS: Find 20 short E words in the story. Circle them.

Pre/Post Test

Directions: Circle all words that have a short vowel sound.

thick	chin	whine	skin
time	chime	twin	mint
will	paid	line	print
dish	swim	side	pride

Directions: Circle the word that will complete each sentence. Write the word on the line.

1. The dog did a _____. tick trick spill

2. We saw the _____ swim in the dish. fist fish fill

3. The _____ may drip on your chin. mite milk mint

4. The kid _____ in the mud. sit slid silk

5. A little pig fell into the _____. drill dig ditch

6. I cut the skin on my _____. wrist rich risk

7. Put the little _____ in the box. chick chin chill

8. Did you put the _____ on the can? lip lid lick

9. Can you see the top of the _____? hit his hill

10. I like to _____ in that pond. swim switch swift

Name _____

Short Vowel Rule:
If a word has only one vowel and it is at the beginning or between consonants, that vowel usually stands for a short sound.

Directions: Say the name of each picture. Draw a circle around its name. Write the word.

1.		fit	fish	fix	_____
2.		drill	drift	ditch	_____
3.		sink	ship	still	_____
4.		bricks	bring	bit	_____
5.		hill	hit	his	_____
6.		chin	chick	chill	_____
7.		wind	wrist	whip	_____
8.		lick	lid	lip	_____

Choose five of the words above and write a sentence for each word.

REMEMBER - If a word has only one vowel and it is between consonants, that vowel usually stands for a short sound.

Directions: Circle each word that has a short I sound. Write the word.

kid _____   stiff _____

chick _____   lift _____

dine _____   time _____

drift _____   shin _____

limb _____   shine _____

line _____   wish _____

Directions: Put a check (✓) by each word that has a short I sound. Write the word.

wrist _____   quick _____

win _____   rich _____

whine _____   rice _____

thin _____   swine _____

fine _____   tip _____

pine _____   skip _____

Directions: Underline each word that has a short I sound. Write the word.

fish _____   slick _____

grid _____   slice _____

grime _____   chill _____

bike _____   spike _____

click _____   skin _____

swim _____   spine _____

Name _____

Directions: Find short I vowel words in the box. Write them on the lines.

bid	wide	limb	slide	fish	kick	mine	site
fit	trick	ride	chin	line	gift	brick	hip
bite	fine	time	kite	drift	lick	pie	ditch
hid	lick	pick	fix	file	split	ink	white

_____   _____   _____

_____   _____   _____

_____

_____

_____

_____

_____

_____

_____   _____   _____

_____   _____   _____

Choose 5 of the words you have written. Write a sentence for each word.

Name _____

Directions: Circle the word that will complete each sentence. Write the word on the line.

1. Do you think the _____ will sink?   sip   ship   spin

2. I will _____ the cup with milk.   fit   fix   fill

3. Will you help me _____ the ditch?   dig   big   bill

4. We sat on the edge of the _____.   cliff   clip   stiff

5. Can you _____ the switch?   fill   flip   skip

6. Her dress is made of _____.   slip   ship   silk

7. I hope you do not _____ your drink.   spin   spill   skill

8. My little dog can do a _____.   trick   trim   twin

9. Do you plan to pay the _____?   drill   bill   still

10. The _____ fell from the tree.   limb   limp   lick

11. Please put the _____ on the bed.   quit   quilt   quick

12. I think I can _____ this ball.   him   his   hit

Name _____

Directions: Put each short I word from the box into correct shape. Then write the word on the line.

print	skin	twin	thin	rich
grit	miss	mink	ditch	pitch
witch	nick	knit	spill	brick
trick	quick	cliff	grip	whip

1. _____

2. _____

3. _____

4. _____

5. _____

6. _____

7. _____

8. _____

9. _____

10. _____

11. _____

12. _____

13. _____

14. _____

15. _____

16. _____

17. _____

18. _____

19. _____

20. _____

Name _____

Directions: Add and subtract letters to find new short I words. Write the words.

1. slick - ck + t   _____

2. drift - ft + ll   _____

3. quick - ck + ll   _____

4. spin - in + ilt   _____

5. swift - ft + tch   _____

6. drink - ink + ift   _____

7. kick - ck + d   _____

8. rich - ch + sk   _____

9. hill - ll + d   _____

10. thick - ck + n   _____

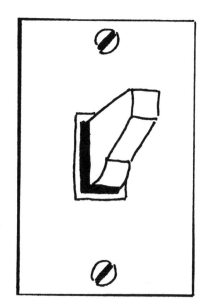

Put the new words you have written in alphabetical order.

1. _____   6. _____

2. _____   7. _____

3. _____   8. _____

4. _____   9. _____

5. _____   10. _____

Directions: Each short I word is written in code. Decode each word, then write the word.

a	b	c	d	e	f	g	h	i	j	k	l	m
1	2	3	4	5	6	7	8	9	10	11	12	13
n	o	p	q	r	s	t	u	v	w	x	y	z
14	15	16	17	18	19	20	21	22	23	24	25	26

1. 16-9-20-3-8 _____

2. 23-9-14-4 _____

3. 23-18-9-19-20 _____

4. 23-8-9-16 _____

5. 12-9-13-16 _____

6. 11-9-19-19 _____

7. 9-14-11 _____

8. 7-9-6-20 _____

9. 23-9-19-8 _____

10. 19-20-9-12-12 _____

11. 3-12-9-6-6 _____

12. 19-16-9-12-12 _____

13. 7-18-9-4 _____

14. 19-11-9-16 _____

15. 20-9-14-20 _____

16. 3-8-9-12-12 _____

Put the words you have written in alphabetical order.

1. _____

2. _____

3. _____

4. _____

5. _____

6. _____

7. _____

8. _____

9. _____

10. _____

11. _____

12. _____

13. _____

14. _____

15. _____

16. _____

Find the words below in the word search puzzle.

```
B Z H I T F M G H J K L L I F T X
I Y Z U F I Z R T N S M O P Q R T
G S T U D V Z I D K K B C D E F I
G H J K L M S N O P I Q R S T U L
L L I F V W X Y Z X Y C D F P I L
H J T B D S M I X O I M I H M N Y
S Q S K I N X V S L I P Y A E E V
K A B C D E F G I H G K L M N O P
I S T U V W X I T Y I N Z X Y Z I
P A R I S K B C D E F G H J K L H
X W D L D W V K C I R B X Y Z D W
J I G L H E F T U F Z R S L M N D
B X Y Z B R Q D G E E T T I U Q A
```

hit	jig	in
fill	quit	him
mix	big	skin
slip	till	lip
skip	whip	dim
brick	it	lift
if	grin	sit
bid	ill	risk

Name _____

Directions: Use each word group in a sentence.

the big ship

1. _____

dig the ditch

2. _____

skin on my lip

3. _____

slip on the hill

4. _____

sit on the cliff

5. _____

fix the switch

6. _____

lift the lid

7. _____

hit him

8. _____

Say these words: ship   silk   spin   slip
Write them in alphabetical order.

1. _____   3. _____

2. _____   4. _____

Name _____

Directions: Write an answer to each riddle. Use words from the box.

quilt	wind	chin	limb	fish
dish	wrist	ship	pig	kid

1. I can swim. What am I? _____

2. I am on a bed. What am I? _____

3. I am on your arm. What am I? _____

4. I am made of glass. What am I? _____

5. I am a baby goat. What am I? _____

6. I am on a tree. What am I? _____

7. I can make a flag wave. What am I? _____

8. I am on your face. What am I? _____

9. I am found on water. What am I? _____

10. I am an animal. What am I? _____

Write all the words In the box In alphabetical order.

1. _____   6. _____

2. _____   7. _____

3. _____   8. _____

4. _____   9. _____

5. _____   10. _____

Name _____

Directions: Find a word in the box to write on the line.

big	brick	kick	swift
sixth	kiss	milk	trick
silk	skip	pig	sick

1. Not water, but _____

2. Not little, but _____

3. Not hug, but _____

4. Not fifth, but _____

5. Not slow, but _____

6. Not wood, but_____

7. Not a cow, but a _____

8. Not well, but _____

9. Not hop, but _____

10. Not a treat, but a _____

11. Not satin, but _____

12. Not punch, but _____

Choose 4 words from the word box. Use each word in a sentence.

1. _____

2. _____

3. _____

4. _____

Directions: Write a synonym (a word that means almost the same) for each word. Use words from the box.

wink	boat	ill	drop	cut
smile	sip	stop	choose	hole
huge	fast	tear	mend	

1. pick _____
2. sick _____
3. grin _____
4. rip _____
5. snip _____
6. spill _____
7. blink _____

8. ship _____
9. drink _____
10. pit _____
11. quit _____
12. big _____
13. fix _____
14. swift _____

Write a sentence for each of these words.

1. wink _____

_____

2. snip _____

_____

3. pit _____

_____

4. swift _____

_____

Directions: Write an antonym (opposite) for each word. Use words from the box.

fat	bright	well	didn't	out
won't	start	frown	stand	lose
hers	slow	break	poor	

1. thin _____

2. grin _____

3. sit _____

4. his _____

5. dim _____

6. fix _____

7. in _____

8. rich _____

9. win _____

10. quick _____

11. did _____

12. quit _____

13. sick _____

14. will _____

Write the short I words in alphabetical order.

1. _____

2. _____

3. _____

4. _____

5. _____

6. _____

7. _____

8. _____

9. _____

10. _____

11. _____

12. _____

13. _____

14. _____

Name _____

Read the story. Then answer the questions.

A little ship drifted down Silver River. It was making a risky trip. A thick mist was hiding tall cliffs on each side of the river.

If it ran into the cliffs, it would be spilled into the river and sink. It would be the ship's last trip if the mist did not lift soon. The night was very still, and the skipper listened to each sound.

At last, it looked as if the mist was thinning. The dim light of the moon slipped through. There were the cliffs right in front of the ship!

The skipper made the wheel spin and the tip of the ship slid past the tall, rocky wall. It was a near miss! Not a split second too soon. Then the mist lifted and he could see! Home at last.

This was a trip he would never forget!

1. What was the name of the river? _____

2. What kind of night was it? _____

3. Why couldn't the skipper see things? _____

4. What was he afraid of hitting? _____

5. How was he able to see the cliffs? _____

6. Did the ship hit the cliff? _____

Read the story. Then answer the questions.

This was the day of the big game! The Winterdale Wimps were playing the Dixon City Drips.

For fifteen years, the Wimps and the Drips had played. The Drips had eight wins and the Wimps had seven. The Wimps wanted to even the wins.

At six o'clock, the starting whistle blew. The game was on! Every play was exciting. Near the end, the score was six to six. The Drips had the ball.

A short pass was flipped to the Drips' end. It hit the tips of his fingers. A Wimp picked it out of the air! The Wimp went spinning for a touchdown! They made the kick for the extra point. The game was over. Final score, 13 to 6.

The Wimps were winners this year — but the Drips will be back.

_____

1. From what town were the Drips? _____

2. From what town were the Wimps? _____

3. How many years had they been playing this game? _____

4. What kind of game was it? _____

5. What was the score when only a few minutes were left? _____

6. What was the final score? _____

7. Who won? _____

Pre/Post Test

Directions: Circle all words that have a short vowel sound.

pond	bone	hope	soap
pool	lost	hop	home
frost	off	drop	not
boss	toad	pot	block

Directions: Circle the word that will complete each sentence. Write the word on the line.

1. The baby took a _____ nap.   **log**   **long**   **lost**

2. We must _____ that bridge.   **cost**   **crop**   **cross**

3. Don and John swam in the _____.   **prong**   **pond**   **prop**

4. How much did the _____ cost?   **smog**   **cloth**   **not**

5. We saw a big _____ by the pond.   **frog**   **fog**   **fond**

6. There is a _____ in my rope.   **lost**   **knock**   **knot**

7. There is a _____ of sheep on the hill.   **sock**   **flock**   **frock**

8. The little girl has _____ her doll.   **lock**   **toss**   **lost**

9. Does the bus _____ on this block?   **stock**   **shop**   **stop**

10. I saw a man _____ the bank.   **rod**   **rob**   **rock**

> **Short Vowel Rule:**
> If a word has only one vowel and it is at the beginning or between consonants, that vowel usually stands for a short sound.

Directions: Say the name of each picture. Draw a circle around its name. Write the word.

1.		chop	clock	crop	_____
2.		rock	rob	rod	_____
3.		blot	box	block	_____
4.		spot	shot	sock	_____
5.		cot	crop	cob	_____
6.		lock	lot	log	_____
7.		mock	mop	moss	_____
8.		frog	frost	fox	_____

Choose five of the words above and write a sentence for each word.

Name _____

REMEMBER - If a word has only one vowel and it is between consonants, that vowel usually stands for a short sound.

Directions: Circle each word that has a short O sound. Write the word.

road _____   loop _____

flop _____   lot _____

stop _____   shot _____

toad _____   room _____

spot _____   snob _____

shop _____   log _____

Directions: Put a check (✓) by each word that has a short O sound. Write the word.

smog _____   road _____

lock _____   shout _____

soup _____   fog _____

jot _____   frog _____

bond _____   hop _____

block _____   float _____

Directions: Underline each word that has a short O sound. Write the word.

lot _____   home _____

plot _____   hot _____

fond _____   load _____

coat _____   drove _____

soil _____   cost _____

frost _____   blot _____

Directions: Find short O vowel words in the box. Write them on the lines.

doll	pond	toast	soap
pop	lot	smog	hot
boat	loaf	frost	boast
cloth	frog	phone	drove
log	rob	home	stock
loan	top	rod	dog
rode	shone	chose	bone
fond	cross	blond	knot

_____ _____

_____ _____

_____ _____

_____ _____

_____ _____

_____ _____

_____ _____

Choose five of the words you have written. Write a sentence for each word.

**Directions: Circle the word that will complete each
sentence. Write the word on the line.**

1.	Tom lost his red _____.	**stop**	**sock**	**stock**
2.	I will help mom _____ the floor.	**mock**	**pom**	**mop**
3.	I hope you don't _____ that glass.	**drop**	**doll**	**stop**
4.	We saw the _____ on the grass.	**fond**	**frost**	**toss**
5.	Don saw a _____ by the pond.	**fog**	**flock**	**frog**
6.	She has blue _____ for her dress.	**cost**	**cloth**	**cross**
7.	We saw a _____ of sheep on the hill.	**flock**	**fog**	**fond**
8.	Put a big _____ in the rope.	**knot**	**knock**	**rod**
9.	There was a loud _____ on the door.	**knock**	**knot**	**nod**
10.	Mr. Ong has a good _____.	**jot**	**job**	**jog**
11.	Please set the _____ on the stove.	**plot**	**pot**	**pod**
12.	You may sleep on that _____.	**clock**	**cot**	**chop**

Write a sentence for each word.

1. chop _____

   _____

2. fond _____

   _____

3. pod _____

   _____

Directions: Put each short O word from the box into its correct shape. Then write the word on the line.

shot	block	sock	odd	lock
knot	smog	stop	not	got
rock	frost	toss	stock	mop
flock	drop	pond	blond	crop

1.  _____

2.  _____

3.  _____

4.  _____

5.  _____

6.  _____

7.  _____

8.  _____

9.  _____

10. _____

11.  _____

12.  _____

13.  _____

14.  _____

15.  _____

16.  _____

17.  _____

18.  _____

19. _____

20. _____

Name _____

Directions: Add and subtract letters to find new short O words. Write the words.

1. block - ck + t   _____

2. log - g + ck   _____

3. frost - st + g   _____

4. lock - ck + g   _____

5. odd - dd + ff   _____

6. pot - t + nd   _____

7. bond - nd + ss   _____

8. shot - t + p   _____

9. chop - hop + lock   _____

10. soft - ft + ck   _____

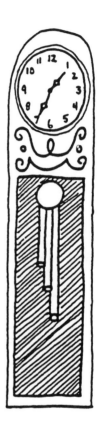

Put the new words you have written in alphabetical order.

1. _____   6. _____

2. _____   7. _____

3. _____   8. _____

4. _____   9. _____

5. _____   10. _____

Directions: Each short O word is written in code. Decode each word, then write the word.

a	b	c	d	e	f	g	h	i	j	k	l	m
1	2	3	4	5	6	7	8	9	10	11	12	13

n	o	p	q	r	s	t	u	v	w	x	y	z
14	15	16	17	18	19	20	21	22	23	24	25	26

1. 18-15-3-11 _____

2. 16-15-14-4 _____

3. 6-12-15-3-11 _____

4. 19-20-15-3-11_____

5. 2-12-15-20 _____

6. 3-8-15-16 _____

7. 19-16-15-20 _____

8. 6-18-15-19-20_____

9. 12-15-19-20 _____

10. 3-18-15-19-19_____

11. 19-13-15-7 _____

12. 10-15-2 _____

13. 3-12-15-3-11 _____

14. 2-15-24 _____

15. 2-15-14-4 _____

16. 3-12-15-20-8 _____

Put the words you have written in alphabetical order.

1. _____

2. _____

3. _____

4. _____

5. _____

6. _____

7. _____

8. _____

9. _____

10. _____

11. _____

12. _____

13. _____

14. _____

15. _____

16. _____

Name _____

Find the words below in the word search puzzle.

```
K A F L O C K D A H O P P Q D T F
N S M N D B M T O S S T R J N R R
O D D P Q L J G A T H L O S T V O
T G R S Y Z T T O P E C D V N Z S
A H T A B E D N O L B S G R A M T
S I H O O L G I Q R X W E Z P E B
O T C R O S S O B L M F A S T F G
F B C D E F G H L J K L F T V P P
T A N Q K C O L O Z H L Y O H U K
V D W T Y Z F O C M A O I C G H C
M A O C H T F R K N N T T K S Z O
X L Y O G T U X E R L A G O Q R R
B O S S A C L O T H N C H H S A M
```

knot	flock	odd
frost	lock	hog
boss	lost	rock
off	blot	rod
soft	cloth	top
block	hop	lot
stock	cross	toss
blond	fog	log

Directions: Use each word group in a sentence.

in the box

1. _____

Tom's sock

2. _____

frog by the pond

3. _____

lost her doll

4. _____

on the log

5. _____

drop the mop

6. _____

lost his job

7. _____

lots of smog

8. _____

Write these words in alphabetical order: blot   soft   block   stock

1. _____   3. _____

2. _____   4. _____

Directions: Fill in each blank with a short O word that rhymes with the underlined word. Choose a word from the box.

cost	box	pot	smog	top
soft	dock	jog	log	cot

1. It is too <u>hot</u> to sleep on that _____.

2. Jane's <u>lost</u> dress _____ a lot of money.

3. There was a <u>lot</u> of soup in the _____.

4. After the rain, the <u>fog</u> and _____ were gone.

5. The bed in the <u>loft</u> was very _____.

6. The boy and his <u>dog</u> liked to_____.

7. They trapped the <u>fox</u> in a_____.

8. There was a <u>clock</u> on the_____.

9. I saw the rabbit <u>hop</u> to the _____ of the hill.

10. There was a <u>frog</u> on the _____.

Write four rhyming words for each of the words below.

got	block	hop	frog
_____	_____	_____	_____
_____	_____	_____	_____
_____	_____	_____	_____
_____	_____	_____	_____

Name _____

Directions: Write a pair of rhyming words in each circle. Use words from the box.

chop	cot	shock
block	rod	shop
hot	moss	frost
cross	lost	pod

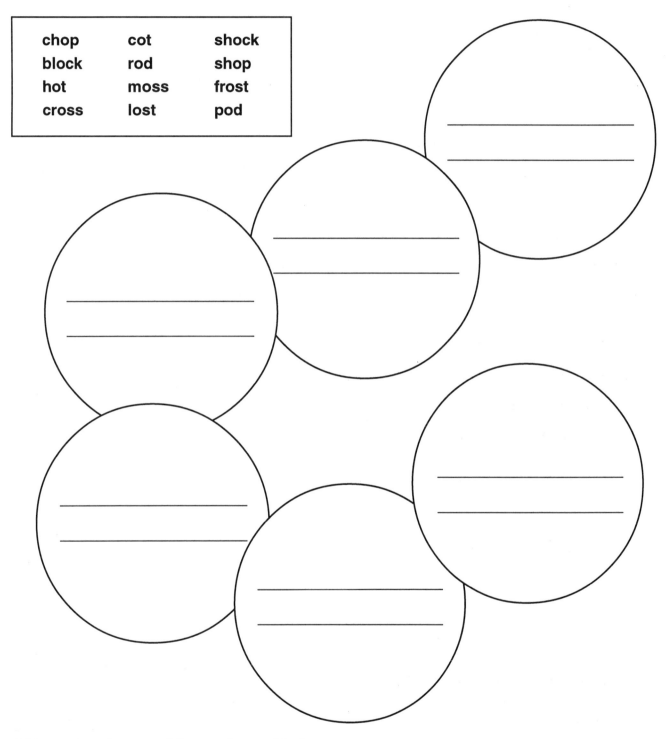

Write a rhyming word for each word below.

1. sock / _____

2. gong / _____

3. gloss / _____

4. mop / _____

Directions: Read each sentence. Find a word in the box that tells what it describes.

pot	ox	frog	dog	smog
knot	frost	sock	doll	hog

1. It is hard to see through. _____

2. It can be seen in winter. _____

3. It likes to hop. _____

4. It likes mud. _____

5. It is a toy. _____

6. It can bark. _____

7. It can hold a plant. _____

8. It can be tied. _____

9. It is a big animal. _____

10. It can be worn on a foot. _____

Write a sentence for each word.

1. clock _____

_____

2. box _____

_____

3. knot _____

_____

Name _____

Step 1: Choose a word from the word box to complete each sentence.

Step 2: Complete each puzzle with the word that you have used in the sentence.

rock	toss	mop	pot	soft
clock	dog	job	flock	shock

1. There was a _____f l o c k_____ of sheep in the field.

2. The mother will _____ the baby to sleep.

3. The maid used a wet _____ on the floor.

4. There was dust on the _____.

5. The dust cloth is very _____.

6. The boy touched the wire and got a _____.

7. I like to _____ the ball into the air.

8. My brother wants to get a _____ as a paperboy.

9. Our _____ is black and white.

10. There was a _____ of stew on the stove.

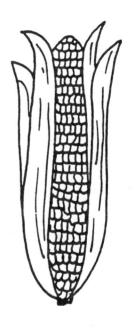

1.
```
  F
  L
B L O C K
  C
  K
```

2.
```
    S
[ ][O][ ]
    C
    K
```

3.
```
  [ ]
H [O] P
  [ ]
```

4. D
```
    O
[C][ ][ ][ ]
    K
```

5.
```
  [ ]
L [O] F T
  [ ]
```

6.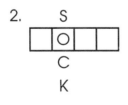
```
      L
[ ][ ][O][ ][ ]
      C
      K
```

7.
```
    B
[ ][O][ ]
    S
    S
```

8.
```
  [ ]
R [O] B
  [ ]
```

9.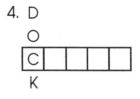
```
    F
[ ][O][ ]
    G
```

10.
```
  [ ]
H [O] T
  [ ]
```

Directions: Find a word in the box to write on the line.

top	blond	chop	sock
frog	mop	tock	soft
pot	fox	off	box

1. Not hard, but _____

2. Not a toad, but a _____

3. Not a redhead, but a _____

4. Not on, but _____

5. Not a pan, but a _____

6. Not a wolf, but a _____

7. Not bottom, but _____

8. Not a broom, but a _____

9. Not a sack, but a _____

10. Not a shoe, but a _____

11. Not tick, but _____

12. Not cut, but _____

Choose 4 words from the word box. Use each word in a sentence.

1. _____

2. _____

3. _____

4. _____

Name _____

Directions: Write a synonym (a word that means almost the same) for each word. Use words from the box.

store	dad	bed	rap
throw	pan	cut	lid
leap	stone	policeman	child
quit	spoil		

1. knock _____

2. rot _____

3. rock _____

4. top _____

5. shop _____

6. toss _____

7. cot _____

8. hop _____

9. chop _____

10. stop _____

11. pop _____

12. cop _____

13. pot _____

14. tot _____

Write the short O words in alphabetical order.

1. _____

2. _____

3. _____

4. _____

5. _____

6. _____

7. _____

8. _____

9. _____

10. _____

11. _____

12. _____

13. _____

14. _____

Name _____

Directions: Write an antonym (opposite) for each word. Use words from the box.

even	on	cold	found	laugh
off	go	bottom	hard	catch

1. odd _____

2. lost _____

3. off _____

4. soft _____

5. on _____

6. sob _____

7. stop _____

8. hot _____

9. toss _____

10. top _____

Write the short O words in alphabetical order.

1. _____

2. _____

3. _____

4. _____

5. _____

6. _____

7. _____

8. _____

9. _____

10. _____

Name _____

Directions: Read the story. Then answer the questions.

Mr. Scroggs' boss was very fond of frog legs. He could eat lots and lots of them for just one meal.

Mr. Scroggs wanted to please his boss. So, one foggy night, he went to the pond. He saw frogs hopping everywhere. But, sitting on a big rock in the middle of the pond was the biggest frog he had ever seen.

The big frog began to sing a croaky song. All the other frogs hopped away into the fog. Scroggs crossed the pond by stepping on rocks. He stopped when he got near the frog. He grabbed the frog's back legs.

He was very shocked when the frog spoke to him. "I am a magic frog," he croaked. "If you set me down and kiss me, you will get a wish."

Scroggs thought about it. "I sure don't want to kiss a frog . . . but, I do want a wish. I'll do it!"

As soon as the frog was set back on the rock, he kicked his strong back legs and hopped away. Scroggs could hear soft, froggy laughs through the fog.

"Maybe," he thought, "I should not try to get something for nothing. Maybe I should just try to do the best job I can."

1. What did Mr. Scroggs' boss like to eat? _____

2. Where did Scroggs go? _____

3. What kind of night was it? _____

4. Where was the big frog sitting? _____

_____

5. What shocked Scroggs? _____

6. What happened to the frog? _____

_____

Directions: Read the story. Then answer the questions.

Once there was a small fox named Boppo. Every day, he trotted down to Farmer Todd's chicken yard. Farmer Todd had a big flock of chickens.

How could he get one? He couldn't knock on Farmer Todd's door and ask for one. A chicken was not going to drop in his paws. The fence was too high to hop over. And Farmer Todd kept the gate locked.

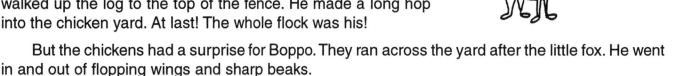

Boppo had an idea! He propped a log up on the fence. He walked up the log to the top of the fence. He made a long hop into the chicken yard. At last! The whole flock was his!

But the chickens had a surprise for Boppo. They ran across the yard after the little fox. He went in and out of flopping wings and sharp beaks.

He made a long jump to the top of the fence. He did not stop running until he got to his nice, soft den. Boppo never trotted near Farmer Todd's chicken yard again!

1. What was the fox's name? _____

2. Who owned the chicken yard? _____

3. Why couldn't Boppo hop over the fence? _____

    _____

4. What did he use to get over? _____

    _____

5. What did the chickens do to Boppo? _____

6. What did the fox do after he got out of the chicken yard? _____

    _____

Pre/Post Test

Directions: Circle all words that have a short vowel sound.

mud	fume	stub	plume
muse	fun	fruit	plum
rule	lunch	nut	tub
slum	tube	stuck	tube

Directions: Circle the word that will complete each sentence. Write the word on the line.

1. We saw the man trim the _____. scrub shrub stub

2. Put the _____ in the sink. punt pug plug

3. They said the ship had _____. sunk skunk shrunk

4. Can you _____ the dog's fur? bunch bust brush

5. Did you sleep in the top _____ ? drunk dunk bunk

6. I think I see _____ on the box. bust dust dumb

7. I hope you can come for _____. lung luck lunch

8. Would you like to eat some _____? munch mush must

9. Did you eat a _____ for lunch? plug plum plump

10. You can ride in the back of the _____. trunk truck tuck

> **Short Vowel Rule:**
> If a word has only one vowel and it is at the beginning or between
> consonants, that vowel usually stands for a short sound.

Directions: Say the name of each picture. Draw a circle around its name. Write the word.

1.		dug	drum	dust	_____
2.		sun	such	shut	_____
3.		just	jug	jut	_____
4.		plug	pump	plum	_____
5.		bug	brush	bud	_____
6.		trunk	tug	truck	_____
7.		hut	hug	hunt	_____
8.		tuck	thump	tub	_____

Choose five of the words above and write a sentence for each word.

Name _____

REMEMBER - If a word has only one vowel and it is between consonants, that vowel usually stands for a short sound.

Directions: Circle each word that has a short U sound. Write the word.

bug	_____	tube	_____
fume	_____	bump	_____
drug	_____	crust	_____
tune	_____	gun	_____
brush	_____	suit	_____
bluff	_____	fruit	_____

Directions: Put a check (✓) by each word that has a short U sound. Write the word.

plum	_____	flute	_____
much	_____	rust	_____
stung	_____	such	_____
plug	_____	stuff	_____
cute	_____	crust	_____
crumb	_____	muse	_____

Directions: Underline each word that has a short U sound. Write the word.

us	_____	bud	_____
tuck	_____	plume	_____
mule	_____	chute	_____
cube	_____	dull	_____
thump	_____	dug	_____
sun	_____	duck	_____

Directions: Find short U vowel words in the box. Write them on the lines.

plug	dug	drum	shrub
prune	true	juice	grub
club	punt	blue	dune
rug	suit	strum	rude
fruit	flute	thump	rut
plum	sun	tube	rule
cruise	spun	dump	cub
chum	blunt	cube	luck

_____   _____

_____   _____

_____   _____

_____   _____

_____   _____

_____   _____

             _____

             _____

             _____

             _____

Choose 5 of the words you have written. Write a sentence for each word.

Name _____

Directions: Put each short U word from the box into its correct shape. Then write the word on the line.

fun	us	tuck	shut	rug
dust	such	crumb	chum	crush
rush	plum	junk	muff	up
much	chump	mud	hung	lunch

1.  _____

2.  _____

3.  _____

4.  _____

5.  _____

6. 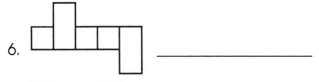 _____

7.  _____

8.  _____

9.  _____

10.  _____

11.  _____

12.  _____

13.  _____

14.  _____

15.  _____

16.  _____

17.  _____

18.  _____

19.  _____

20.  _____

Name _____

Directions: Add and subtract letters to find new short U words. Write the words.

1. lunch - nch + mp   _____

2. thumb - b + p   _____

3. such - ch + m   _____

4. bug - g + mp   _____

5. crumb - mb + st   _____

6. duck - ck + st   _____

7. hung - g + t   _____

8. dug - g + ll   _____

9. much - ch + g   _____

10. mush - h + t   _____

Put the new words you have written in alphabetical order.

1. _____   6. _____

2. _____   7. _____

3. _____   8. _____

4. _____   9. _____

5. _____   10. _____

Directions: Each short U word is written in code. Decode each word, then write the word.

a	b	c	d	e	f	g	h	i	j	k	l	m
1	2	3	4	5	6	7	8	9	10	11	12	13

n	o	p	q	r	s	t	u	v	w	x	y	z
14	15	16	17	18	19	20	21	22	23	24	25	26

1. 2-21-14-3-8 _____

2. 19-16-18-21-14-7 _____

3. 7-18-21-14-20 _____

4. 2-12-21-19-8 _____

5. 19-20-18-21-20 _____

6. 19-3-18-21-2 _____

7. 8-21-14-3-8 _____

8. 12-21-14-3-8 _____

9. 19-16-21-14 _____

10. 19-20-21-13-16 _____

11. 16-12-21-7 _____

12. 19-20-21-2 _____

13. 3-12-21-3-11 _____

14. 3-12-21-2 _____

15. 20-18-21-19-20 _____

16. 14-21-20 _____

Put the words you have written in alphabetical order.

1. _____

2. _____

3. _____

4. _____

5. _____

6. _____

7. _____

8. _____

9. _____

10. _____

11. _____

12. _____

13. _____

14. _____

15. _____

16. _____

Name _____

Find the words below in the word search puzzle.

```
R U S H L L U M P N C E R Q S
R S K N D B O Y S E E H U S H
H F U R H S U R B T H N N U U
U G L S Y Z T A Z P E C U V T
G H L U C K I N U L A S S R F
C I H O O F G I Q R B U T Z U
H U T A F K B O B L M F A S S
U B C U E F G M U L P L M N S
S A P Q R G A S G T H M F C H
K D W R B N S O O S T U C K G
M A T C H T K R R M N D T A S
C L U M P T U S U C H K C U D
```

shut	puff	brush
rush	bug	mud
stuck	clump	but
run	up	duck
fuss	lump	hug
such	skull	hut
husk	plum	sun
luck	hush	fun

Name _____

Directions: Use each word group in a sentence.

stuck in the mud

1. _____

jump in the tub

2. _____

gum on the rug

3. _____

plum for lunch

4. _____

bug on the stump

5. _____

duck by the truck

6. _____

skunk by the shrub

7. _____

dust on the drum

8. _____

Write these words in alphabetical order: **bug   buck   dust   dump**

1. _____   3. _____

2. _____   4. _____

Name _____

Directions: Write a pair of rhyming words in each circle. Use words from the box.

scrub	truck	drum	chum	flush	smug	punt
stunt	plug	stuck	thump	club	plump	blush

Write a rhyming word for each word below.

1. lump / _____

2. rub / _____

3. mush / _____

4. rug / _____

5. plum / _____

6. munch / _____

Name _____

Step 1: Choose a word from the word box to complete each sentence below.

Step 2: Complete each puzzle with the word that you have used in the sentence.

crust	bump	dust	tub	brush
hung	dug	bus	sun	hunt

1. Ann left the water running in the ____t u b____ .

2. The bat _____ upside down from the tree.

3. The _____ on the apple pie was crisp.

4. Spot _____ a hole in the backyard.

5. My comb and _____ need washing.

6. Sam likes to _____ for deer.

7. Please don't _____ into the rose bush.

8. I hope the _____ will shine today!

9. Mother told me to _____ the table.

10. Jim wanted to take the _____ to school.

1.
```
     L
   T U B
     C
     K
```

2.
```
   □
 S U N G
   □
   □
```

3.
```
     M
 □ □ U □ □
     S
     T
```

4.
```
   □
 M U G
   □
```

5.
```
     R
 □ □ U □
     S
     T
```

6.
```
   H
 □ U □
   N
   G
```

7.
```
   □
 S T U M P
   □
   □
```

8.
```
   S
 □ U □
   C
   H
```

9.
```
 □
 T U C K
 □
```

10.
```
   D
 □ U □
   L
   L
```

83

Name _____

Directions: Find a word in the box to write on the line.

lunch	gum	sun	brush
plum	thumb	hug	run
hum	shrub	bus	duck

1. Not walk, but _____

2. Not dinner, but _____

3. Not candy, but _____

4. Not a finger, but a _____

5. Not a comb, but a _____

6. Not a goose, but a _____

7. Not a peach, but a _____

8. Not sing, but _____

9. Not a tree, but a _____

10. Not the moon, but the _____

11. Not a kiss, but a _____

12. Not a train, but a _____

Choose 4 words from the word box. Use each word in a sentence.

1. _____

2. _____

3. _____

4. _____

Name _____

Directions: Write a synonym (a word that means almost the same) for each word. Use words from the box.

insect	bed	close	fat
hit	dollar	dirt	leap
cozy	friend	cup	bottle
pull	eat		

1. bug _____

2. bunk _____

3. dust _____

4. jug _____

5. shut _____

6. tug _____

7. jump _____

8. punch _____

9. buck _____

10. mug _____

11. snug _____

12. chum _____

13. plump _____

14. munch _____

Write the short U words in alphabetical order.

1. _____

2. _____

3. _____

4. _____

5. _____

6. _____

7. _____

8. _____

9. _____

10. _____

11. _____

12. _____

13. _____

14. _____

Directions: Some of the words in the box name "things." Write each word that names a thing you could touch.

tub	trunk	dumb	mud
nut	truck	must	bus
much	rug	gun	bump
plump	up	drum	dull
such	skunk	sunk	dust

1. _____

2. _____

3. _____

4. _____

5. _____

6. _____

7. _____

8. _____

9. _____

10. _____

11. _____

12. _____

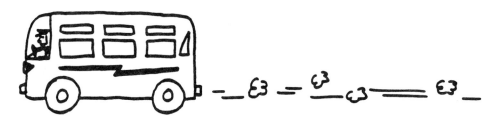

Choose 3 words from the box. Use each in a sentence.

1. _____

_____

2. _____

_____

3. _____

_____

Read the story. Answer the questions.

Pug Mullen was a truck driver. One day he was in a rush to take a load of nuts to the Crunchy Candy Factory.

His truck was humming along the road when Pug heard a funny clunk under the hood. "What crummy luck," thought Pug. "Something must be wrong."

Pug stopped off the side of the road and jumped out to see. The sun was hot, and it was dusty by the road. Pug felt grumpy.

He looked under the hood and saw that a rusty nut had come loose. He fixed the nut and shut the hood. He jumped back into his truck. But he did not go anywhere. He was stuck in the deep dirt! One tire was up to the hubcap in dust.

Just then a big bus came along. It stopped and some men got off the bus to help Pug. They dug the stuff away so the truck could roll back onto the road. Pug thanked the men very much and buzzed off to the Crunchy Candy Factory.

1. What kind of job did Pug have?

   _____

2. What was he carrying in his truck?

   _____

3. Where was he going?

   _____

4. Why did he stop by the side of the road?

   _____

5. Who came along to help him?

   _____

Read the story. Answer the questions.

Bucky and Buddy made a clubhouse. They named their club the "Thumbs Up" club. Holding thumbs up was their secret sign.

They hunted around the old dump for stuff they could use. They found lots of good junk there. They found a rug they could use for the floor and a big tub to use for a chair. They also got an old trunk to make a table.

The boys dug a hole in one corner. They could tuck secret stuff in it. On Saturday mornings they would bring a jug of lemonade and paper cups to the clubhouse. They would even eat lunch there. They let Chuck join the club. He had an old shutter. They hung it over the doorway. They could open and shut it to see if anyone was near.

The boys had lots of fun in the clubhouse.

1. Who made a clubhouse?

   _____

2. What did they name the club?

   _____

3. What did they find to use as a table?

   _____

4. Why did they dig a hole in the corner?

   _____

5. Who else joined the club?

   _____

Name _____

Pre/Post Test

Directions: Circle all words that have a short vowel sound.

them	home	thin	fled
stop	tube	whine	win
glass	tub	best	stone
place	flat	lake	club

Directions: Circle the word that will complete each sentence. Write the word on the line.

1. I hope you don't _____ your bus. **mess   miss   moss**

2. Put this big _____ on the box. **strap   stop   step**

3. The little dog has food in his _____. **dash   bush   dish**

4. Please turn on the _____. **limp   lamp   lump**

5. My truck is _____ in the mud. **stuck   stack   stick**

6. The eggs will _____ very soon. **hitch   hutch   hatch**

7. We put the _____ in the pen. **limp   lamb   bump**

8. Is your book on the _____? **shift   shelf   shock**

9. My leg is very _____. **stuff   stiff   staff**

10. His lunch is in that _____. **stuck   sick   sack**

Name _____

REMEMBER - If a word has only one vowel and it is between consonants, that vowel usually stands for a short sound.

Directions: Circle each word that has a short vowel sound. Write the word.

toad	_____	time	_____
flop	_____	split	_____
step	_____	flub	_____
flat	_____	mate	_____
_____		shin	_____
stub	_____	home	_____
		plot	_____

Directions: Put a check (✓) by each word that has a short vowel sound. Write the word.

rag	_____	soap	_____
clock	_____	bean	_____
tone	_____	pin	_____
stab	_____	tag	_____
bench	_____	bust	_____
bake	_____	spine	_____

Directions: Underline each word that has a short vowel sound. Write the word.

best	_____	chase	_____
fin	_____	tube	_____
tub	_____	fine	_____
glad	_____	black	_____
bone	_____	test	_____
top	_____	shop	_____

Directions: Circle short vowel words in the box. Write them on the lines.

shop	sped	drop	ride	bled	cape
stack	rate	tube	state	skip	rub
best	much	rat	thin	stub	check
mice	spend	hose	mop	flag	peel
cap	skin	cheek	home	plate	seat
slid	hunt	brick	tub	soap	chop
block	bake	crate	tune	twice	flap

SHORT A

_____

_____

_____

_____

_____

SHORT E

_____

_____

_____

_____

_____

SHORT I

_____

_____

_____

_____

_____

SHORT O

_____

_____

_____

_____

SHORT U

_____

_____

_____

_____

Name _____

Directions: Circle the word that will complete each sentence. Write the word on the line.

1.	The man's car was _____ in the mud.	stick stack stuck
2.	I will _____ you if you go.	miss mess muss
3.	You can help me _____ logs.	chap chip chop
4.	I saw a red _____ in that shop.	lump lamp limp
5.	The big _____ sat in the tree.	champ chump chimp
6.	That's a big _____ for such a little fish!	fan fin fun
7.	I will use the _____ to scrub the spot.	rug rag rig
8.	My dog likes to sleep on the _____.	bad bud bed
9.	The little _____ can eat the seeds.	chuck chick check
10.	That big _____ can jump the fence.	lamb limb lamp
11.	The black dog _____ the little boy.	bet bat bit
12.	I sat in the sun and got a _____.	ten tan tin

Write the words you circled in alphabetical order.

1. _____   7. _____

2. _____   8. _____

3. _____   9. _____

4. _____   10. _____

5. _____   11. _____

6. _____   12. _____

Name _____

Directions: Put each short vowel word from the box into its correct shape. Then write the word on the line.

cliff	spell	trim	twin	bell	bunch	spot
chest	trunk	club	glass	quilt	patch	smell
duck	sock	egg	knot	glad	chop	

1. 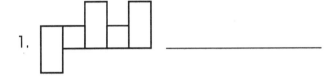 _____

2.  _____

3.  _____

4.  _____

5.  _____

6.  _____

7.  _____

8.  _____

9. 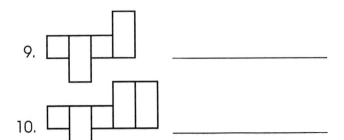 _____

10. 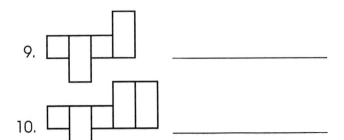 _____

11.  _____

12.  _____

13.  _____

14.  _____

15.  _____

16.  _____

17. _____

18. _____

19. _____

20. _____

Name _____

Directions: Fill in each blank with a short vowel word that rhymes with the underlined word. Choose a word from the box.

sun	cash	dish	grass
shed	shop	pin	fell

1. There is a broken <u>glass</u> on the _____.

2. Santa keeps his <u>sled</u> in a _____.

3. You can get a <u>pop</u> in the _____.

4. I <u>wish</u> I had a _____ of fruit.

5. We are going to have <u>fun</u> in the _____.

6. I will be back in a <u>flash</u> with the _____.

7. He heard the girl <u>yell</u> as she _____.

8. Please do not <u>spin</u> the _____.

Write four rhyming words for each of the words below.

chin   **cab**   **bed**

_____ _____ _____

_____ _____ _____

_____ _____ _____

_____ _____ _____

stop   **bum**

_____ _____

_____ _____

_____ _____

_____ _____

Directions: Choose the correct blend to make a word in each box.

1.		2.		3.	
gr		tr		gr	
sn	__ __ ack	fl	__ __ ell	bl	__ __ in
sp		sh		st	

4.		5.		6.	
sp		ch		bl	
sw	__ __ ip	tr	__ __ um	tr	__ __ uck
sh		bl		sp	

7.		8.	
tr		fr	
gr	__ __ ock	br	__ __ anch
cl		sp	

Directions: Use words in the boxes to write the correct answer on the line.

1. a friend _____   5. part of an egg _____

2. a smile _____   6. has four wheels _____

3. tells time _____   7. part of a tree _____

4. moves in water _____   8. something to eat _____

Directions: Circle the short vowel words in the big box. Write the words in the correct small boxes.

ham	hid	seen	tune	pot
tip	rage	nut	robe	red
hop	hen	feel	mule	bun
rag	rob	pine	mad	bell
rut	pin	home	sleep	hide

SHORT A

_____

_____

_____

SHORT E

_____

_____

_____

SHORT I

_____

_____

_____

SHORT O

_____

_____

_____

SHORT U

_____

_____

_____

Choose 3 words from the box. Write a sentence for each word.

Step 1: Choose a word from the word box to complete each sentence below.

Step 2: Complete each puzzle with the word that you have used in the sentence.

cab	dust	spend	rust	branch
odd	shed	hatch	fresh	silk

1. There still are some leaves on the _____ b r a n c h _____.

2. Please phone for a _____.

3. I like _____ cut flowers.

4. My mother wants me to clean the _____.

5. There is an _____ smell in the house.

6. Some of my mother's plants are made from _____.

7. There is _____ all over the table.

8. I had to rub to get all the _____ off my bike.

9. The chicken's egg will _____ soon.

10. How long will it take you to _____ a dollar?

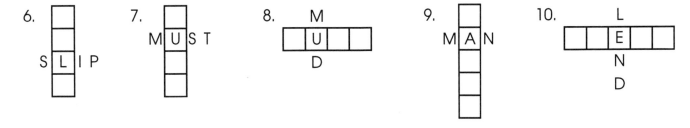

Name _____

Directions: Draw a line from a word in List 1 to a word in List 2 to make a compound word.

List 1	List 2
bath	stop
back	cloth
egg	tub
dish	plant
drum	stick
egg	cuff
hand	nog
hill	top

Directions: Write a sentence for each compound word you have made.

1. _____

2. _____

3. _____

4. _____

5. _____

6. _____

7. _____

8. _____

Directions: Draw a line from a word in List 1 to a word in List 2 to make a compound word.

List 1   List 2

cat   hand

egg   man

dust   fish

gun   up

pick   pan

back   set

hand   shell

up   gun

Directions: Write a sentence for each compound word you have made.

1. _____

2. _____

3. _____

4. _____

5. _____

6. _____

7. _____

8. _____

Name _____

Directions: Fill in each blank with a compound word. Use words from the box.

dishcloth	pickup	upset	drumstick
gunmen	bathtub	eggshell	catfish

1. I ate a _____ for lunch.

2. The green _____ was stuck In the mud.

3. Wipe the table with the _____.

4. He saw a _____ in the pond.

5. My dad was _____ when he saw the mess.

6. The two _____ ran from the bank.

7. There is a crack in the _____.

8. It is your turn to scrub the _____.

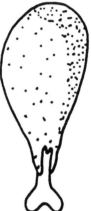

Directions: Divide the words in the box into syllables.

1. _____ / _____   5. _____ / _____

2. _____ / _____   6. _____ / _____

3. _____ / _____   7. _____ / _____

4. _____ / _____   8. _____ / _____

Choose three words from the box. Write a sentence for each word.

1. _____

2. _____

3. _____

100

Write a story. Use as many of the short vowel words from the box as you can. Give your story a title. Draw a picture about your story in the space.

class	print	rush	his	clock
test	spell	pen	bell	lunch

(Title) _____

_____

_____

_____

_____

_____

_____

_____

_____

_____

_____

_____

_____

_____

_____

_____

_____

Name _____

Directions: Read the story. Then answer the questions. Write your answers in complete sentences.

Frogs live in ponds. When they feel a chill in the air, they dig a hole in the soft mud at the bottom of the pond. They take in air through their skin. When the days get warm, they swim to the top again.

Frogs lay eggs near the top of the water. The baby frog is much like a fish at first. It breathes with gills and uses its fins to swim. Then it gets legs and its tail falls off.

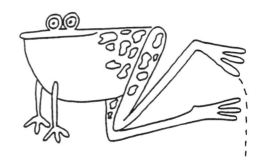

Frogs can hop on land, but they stay near water. This way they can keep their skin wet. If their skin gets too dry, the frog will die. Frogs eat bugs that are near the pond. They can jump very far and very fast. It is no easy trick to catch a frog.

1. Where do frogs live?

    _____

2. What do they do when it gets cold?

    _____

3. When do they come back to the top?

    _____

4. Where do frogs lay their eggs?

    _____

5. What is a baby frog like at first?

    _____

6. Why do frogs stay near water?

    _____

Directions: Read the story. Then answer the questions.

Dad and Jack went on a camping trip. When they got to the camping spot, they unpacked the truck.

Jack helped Dad set up the tent and got out the sleeping bags. Then he went to find twigs and logs for a fire.

When the camp was set up, they got their rods to go fishing. It was a short trip over the hill to the stream. Jack sat quietly until he felt a tug. It was a big fish. It would make a good dinner.

They had six fish when they left to go back to camp. As they followed the path, they met a skunk. "Shhhh," said Dad. "Just let him go past. That is one smell we can do without."

Dad chopped the logs and made a fire. Dinner was great. Then they got into their snug sleeping bags. Tomorrow they would hunt and fish all day.

As Jack shut his eyes, he thought how lucky he was to have such a swell dad.

1. How did Jack and his dad get to the camping spot?

    _____

2. What did Jack help his dad do first?

    _____

3. Who gathered twigs for the fire? _____

4. How many fish did they catch? _____

5. What did they meet on the path? _____

6. Why did Jack think he was lucky?

    _____

Directions: Read the story. Then answer the questions.

Billy the Squid lives in the deep, blue sea. He spends his time sifting the sand looking for tidbits to munch. With his eight long arms, he can grab a lot of snacks — and lunch, too.

Sometimes he passes the time with his pals. Cal Crab and Sam Clam. They cannot swim as fast as Billy. But they can hide in the rocks better. When they play tag, Sam's shell keeps him from ever being "it." He shuts it and no one can tag him!

When they run races, Cal can go fast on his six legs. When they swim, Billy is always the winner.

They know to sit very still in the tall sea grass when they see the big fin of a shark. Once the big tail swishes by, they swim out for more fun.

1. What is the squid's name? _____

2. How many arms does he have? _____

3. Who are his friends?

   _____

4. How does Sam keep from being tagged?

   _____

5. Who wins at swimming? _____

6. When do they sit very still?

   _____

Pre/Post Test

Directions: Circle all words that have a long vowel sound.

coax	shin	leave	float	check
prize	steam	cute	scrap	wheeze
scrap	throat	shine	throw	shrub
chain	stay	flat	step	phone

Directions: Circle the word that will complete each sentence. Write the word on the line.

1. The girl had a _____ in her hair.   **bred**   **braid**   **brad**

2. We will plant a _____ tree.   **pine**   **pin**   **pain**

3. We saw _____ on the water.   **fame**   **foam**   **fine**

4. A little _____ sat on the road.   **tide**   **tame**   **toad**

5. The _____ walked down the road.   **mile**   **mail**   **mule**

6. I _____ to clean my room.   **hate**   **hat**   **hot**

7. Put the _____ in the cup.   **cram**   **claim**   **cream**

8. What _____ does the bell ring?   **time**   **tin**   **team**

9. We smelled _____ in the air.   **fame**   **farms**   **fumes**

If a word with one syllable has two vowels, the first vowel usually stands for a long sound and the second vowel is silent.

Example: ra̅i̸n   pla̅y̸   sa̅ve̸

Directions: Say the name of each picture. Draw a circle around its name. Write the word.

1.	tray	train	trap
2.	plate	plan	play
3.	map	maid	mad
4.	leap	lay	lake
5.	crāte	crab	clay
6.	claim	cāve	cane
7.	hāy	hāve	had
8.	clay	chain	cab

Choose five of the words above and write a sentence for each word.

Name _____

Directions: Circle the word that will complete each sentence.
Write the word on the line.

1. The monkey was in a _____ at the zoo.   **cake**   **cage**   **crab**

2. My dad will _____ the house red.   **paint**   **pay**   **pad**

3. What _____ will you be in next year?   **gate**   **grade**   **grab**

4. The _____ has been late for two days.   **main**   **mad**   **mail**

5. I like to play in the _____.   **sad**   **sail**   **shade**

6. May I see your _____ ring?   **jade**   **jail**   **jab**

7. John's _____ is very dirty.   **fade**   **fast**   **face**

8. How much will I be _____ to cut the grass?   **pave**   **paid**   **pad**

9. Mary made a long, red _____.   **cape**   **case**   **cap**

10. Please don't _____ me for the mess.   **brain**   **back**   **blame**

11. How long will it take to _____ the cake?   **back**   **bake**   **bray**

12. I like to _____ in the park.   **scale**   **stack**   **skate**

Write the words you circled in alphabetical order.

1. _____   7. _____

2. _____   8. _____

3. _____   9. _____

4. _____   10. _____

5. _____   11. _____

6. _____   12. _____

If a word with one syllable has two vowels, the first vowel usually stands for a long sound and the second vowel is silent.

Example: seen   seam

Directions: Say the name of each picture. Draw a circle around its name. Write the word.

1.		bet	bent	beet	_____
2.		seal	seed	set	_____
3.		fed	fad	feet	_____
4.		beak	beach	bet	_____
5.		well	wheel	wade	_____
6.		pet	peach	pen	_____
7.		heap	hem	heel	_____
8.		leak	leaf	left	_____

Choose five of the words above and write a sentence for each word.

Name _____

Directions: Circle the word that will complete each sentence.
Write the word on the line.

1. That big frog can _____ over the log.   **lead**   **leap**   **left**

2. Please don't _____ that drum!   **bet**   **bell**   **beat**

3. We saw a big _____ on the rock.   **sell**   **seal**   **seem**

4. I like to take a _____ bath.   **stem**   **steel**   **steam**

5. We like to wade in the _____.   **steal**   **stream**   **stem**

6. Please _____ me after school.   **met**   **mean**   **meet**

7. That trail is very _____.   **steep**   **step**   **send**

8. I think I ate the _____.   **seat**   **seed**   **see**

9. I will put the _____ on the bed.   **step**   **sheet**   **sheen**

10. Did you eat all the _____?   **met**   **meat**   **mend**

11. I did not _____ to get in your way.   **meat**   **mean**   **met**

12. There is a cool _____ at night.   **breeze**   **bet**   **breed**

Write a sentence for each word below.

1. steep _____

2. steel _____

3. mean _____

4. leap _____

            PHONICS

If a word with one syllable has two vowels, the first vowel usually stands for a long sound and the second vowel is silent.

Example: li̶e̶   pi̅ne̶

Directions: Say the name of each picture. Draw a circle around its name. Write the word.

#					
1.		tip	tie	tide	_____
2.		file	fill	fail	_____
3.		pie	pile	pain	_____
4.		slid	skid	slide	_____
5.		die	dime	dim	_____
6.		tire	tried	train	_____
7.		kid	kit	kite	_____
8.		lain	lime	lid	_____

Choose five of the words above and write a sentence for each word.

Name _____

Directions: Circle the word that will complete each sentence.
Write the word on the line.

1. I would like to buy _____ new pencils.   **five**   first   fit

2. The _____ of that dog is huge.   **slip**   side   size

3. Jim walked a _____ to school.   **mint**   mine   mile

4. Please _____ your name on your paper.   **write**   wrist   wide

5. It will cost a _____ to buy some candy.   **die**   dime   dine

6. Mary is going on a _____ today.   **hill**   hike   hide

7. What is the _____ of the coat?   **price**   prize   print

8. The lady's new dress was _____.   **wine**   wind   white

9. Joe is going to _____ off the table.   **with**   wipe   wide

10. A train _____ can be fun.   **rid**   ride   ripe

11. Can you _____ your shoelace?   **tin**   tie   time

12. There is a _____ of rocks on the street.   **pine**   pile   pill

Write a rhyming word for each word below.

1. fine   _____   5. tile   _____

2. bike   _____   6. ripe   _____

3. rice   _____   7. hide   _____

4. hive   _____   8. lime   _____

Name _____

If a word with one syllable has two vowels, the first vowel usually stands for a long sound and the second vowel is silent.

Example: bo̅a̶t   to̅e̶

Directions: Say the name of each picture. Draw a circle around its name. Write the word.

#	Picture	Choices	Write
1.		bat boat beat	_____
2.		who her hoe	_____
3.		got goat gold	_____
4.		cop cope coat	_____
5.		blot bow blow	_____
6.		toast toss torch	_____
7.		look loaf lot	_____
8.		doll do doe	_____

Choose five of the words above and write a sentence for each word.

Name _____

Directions: Circle the word that will complete each sentence.
Write the word on the line.

1. We fed _____ to the horse.   **oak**   **odd**   **oats**

2. Did you stub your _____ on the step?   **toe**   **top**   **too**

3. I want to _____ you my new car.   **shop**   **show**   **soap**

4. The little _____ was with her mother.   **doe**   **do**   **dot**

5. Please put the _____ in the pen.   **got**   **goat**   **goal**

6. I got a _____ grade on my test.   **lode**   **loaf**   **low**

7. May I have jam on my _____?   **toast**   **toss**   **toes**

8. Let's plant a seed and watch it _____.   **go**   **grope**   **grow**

9. The _____ was very slick.   **roll**   **rod**   **road**

10. You may sit in the first _____.   **rose**   **row**   **rope**

11. Will that hat _____ on the water?   **float**   **fold**   **frost**

12. The man shot an arrow from his _____.   **bone**   **bowl**   **bow**

Choose four of the words you have circled. Use each word in a sentence.

1. _____

_____

2. _____

_____

3. _____

_____

4. _____

_____

If a word with one syllable has two vowels, the first vowel usually stands for a long sound and the second vowel is silent.

Example: stoné   cuté

Directions: Say the name of each picture. Draw a circle around its name. Write the word.

1.		row	rose	rob
2.		fuse	fuzz	fuss
3.		coon	cone	cob
4.		mule	mud	must
5.		cub	cup	cube
6.		blond	bone	boat
7.		noose	note	nose
8.		phone	poke	pond

Choose five of the words above and write a sentence for each word.

©Remedia Publications

Name _____

Directions: Put each long vowel word from the box into its correct shape.
Then write the word on the line.

nose	hit	mule	live	bell
shop	spot	cliff	can	slide
toad	sail	mud	pray	glass
sat	pin	bleed	knot	egg

1.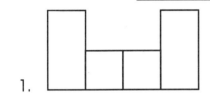

_____

2.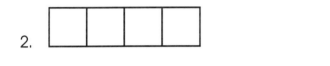

_____

3.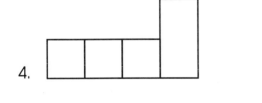

_____

4.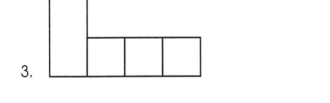

_____

5.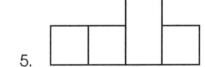

_____

6.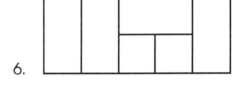

_____

7.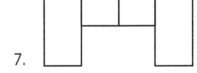

_____

8.

_____

Choose four long vowel words from above. Write a sentence for each one.

1. _____

2. _____

3. _____

4. _____

Directions: Circle the long vowel words in the box. Write the words you circled in the correct shape below.

row	hide	hid	throat	save
bent	map	kit	hop	seed
beat	rent	soap	chain	kite
fine	cream	pot	line	fin
play	sail	thin	please	bone

LONG A

_____

_____

_____

_____

LONG E

_____

_____

_____

_____

LONG I

_____

_____

_____

_____

LONG O

_____

_____

_____

_____

Choose three long vowel words from the box. On a separate sheet of paper, write a sentence for each word.

116

Directions: Circle each word that has a long vowel sound. Write the word.

land _____   braid _____

melt _____   tow _____

mule _____   meal _____

screen _____   lost _____

pray _____   tie _____

fill _____   toast _____

Directions: Put a check (✓) by each word that has a long vowel sound. Write the word.

coat _____   maid _____

cot _____   weld _____

streak _____   mill _____

stack _____   mile _____

crumb _____   made _____

stay _____   feast _____

Directions: Underline each word that has a long vowel sound. Write the word.

chain _____   rest _____

file _____   bake _____

toe _____   cream _____

lint _____   must _____

flock _____   fume _____

roast _____   blow _____

Directions: Choose the correct homonym for each sentence. Write it in the blank.

meat — meet

1. I would like to _____ you after school.

2. That _____ is very good.

3. Please _____ me at 5 o'clock.

heal — heel

1. The _____ of her foot was sore.

2. The _____ on my shoe is worn out.

3. My knee will _____ soon.

week — weak

1. I will help you paint next _____.

2. Sue is not strong; she is _____.

3. There are seven days in a _____.

pail — pale

1. Fill the _____ with some sand.

2. Tom looks very _____.

3. Put the plum in the _____.

road — rode

1. John _____ his bike to school.

2. She _____ her horse into the barn.

3. The _____ was closed for a week.

maid — made

1. The _____ took the day off.

2. I _____ a red dress.

3. Mother _____ a peach pie for me.

Name _____

13 - 9 - 3 - 5

Directions: Each long vowel word is written in code.
Decode each word, then write the word.

a	b	c	d	e	f	g	h	i	j	k	l	m
1	2	3	4	5	6	7	8	9	10	11	12	13

n	o	p	q	r	s	t	u	v	w	x	y	z
14	15	16	17	18	19	20	21	22	23	24	25	26

1. 3-18-15-1-11 _____

2. 3-18-9-13-5 _____

3. 2-5-5-6 _____

4. 19-5-1-13 _____

5. 20-8-5-19-5 _____

6. 2-18-1-9-14 _____

7. 7-1-9-14 _____

8. 3-12-15-19-5 _____

9. 13-15-23 _____

10. 19-12-1-20-5 _____

11. 23-8-9-12-5 _____

12. 3-21-20-5 _____

13. 15-23-14 _____

14. 16-9-5 _____

15. 19-23-5-5-16 _____

16. 18-5-5-6 _____

Put the words you have written in alphabetical order.

1. _____

2. _____

3. _____

4. _____

5. _____

6. _____

7. _____

8. _____

9. _____

10. _____

11. _____

12. _____

13. _____

14. _____

15. _____

16. _____

Name _____

Find the words below in the word search puzzle.

```
R F S G H D W O R C N I K F S G R L
B D T Y L M H K A B R C L V H K D E
A B R C D E I F G H I A J K L M N U
O P A Q R S L T U V E W X Y Z E O F
S H I N E J E I B R O A M D C A X I
P R N O T U V W I Z F R D V O P Q R
O L J R V I B D O W X A B Y A R T D
K T V U A L E A V E S N M A L E I F
E S R V X A L M N E O P Q R M S T U
Q P L T E I X B C K T O N A I F D V
R O I I B A N Q D F G H R I J A B W
K L M E N O A B E D S F U M E Z Y X
```

coal	crow	foe
spoke	fume	week
shine	while	frame
tie	leaves	tray
fuel	real	strain

Name _____

Directions: Fill in the puzzle below with words from the box. Use the clues.

smoke	vine	pine	rose	leaves
green	heel	eel	cone	write

1. ___ ___ ___ **L**

2. ___ **O** ___ ___

3. ___ ___ **N** ___

4. **G** ___ ___ ___ ___

5. **V** ___ ___ ___

6. ___ **O** ___ ___

7. **W** ___ ___ ___ ___

8. **E** ___ ___

9. **L** ___ ___ ___ ___ ___

10. **S** ___ ___ ___ ___

CLUES:

1. it is part of your foot

2. a kind of flower

3. a type of tree

4. a color

5. grapes grow on this

6. something that holds ice cream

7. you do this with a pencil

8. a fish shaped like a snake

9. they grow on a tree

10. it comes out of a chimney

Choose five of the words above and write a sentence for each word.

Name _____

LONG A E I O U

Read the story. Then answer the questions below.

Mr. Dole is known for his fine garden and beautiful yard. He spends whole days weeding, mowing, hoeing, spading, and sowing seeds.

Daisies line the driveway, and sweet peas grow on the wire fence. White lilies fill a whole corner. Mr. Dole takes pride in his prize-winning roses. He likes to show them to people. He smiles at the praise they get.

His grapevines have deep, green leaves. They are loaded with sweet fruit. Bees buzz around the peach tree. An oak tree shades the yard. Rain keeps the grass green and thick.

Neat rows of beans grow on poles. Stakes hold the plants with ripe tomatoes, ready to eat.

Mr. Dole keeps on the trail of snails that like to feast on his plants. Sometimes, bugs creep in to make a meal in his garden.

It took a long time for Mr. Dole to grow all his plants. He knows how to keep them alive and in good shape.

_____
_____

1. What is Mr. Dole known for? _____

2. How does he spend his days? _____

    _____

3. What kind of flowers grow on the wire fence? _____

4. Name two vegetable plants that grow in Mr. Dole's garden.

    _____

5. Mr. Dole doesn't like snails. Why not? _____

    _____

Name _____

Read the story. Then answer the questions below.

Each Friday, Miss Lane has her class name the books they have been reading, and speak on what they were about.

Gail gave the first speech. She had read "Snow White" to her little sister, Joan. Joan now knows the names of all seven dwarfs.

Jay spoke about a tale about a five-mile bike race that nine riders tried to win at a state fair. One rode over a nail and got a flat tire. Another broke a wheel. The slowest racer lost his chain. Only five came over the finish line.

The name of Wade's book was "Space Race." Planes streaked after each other at high speeds. Smoke and flames came from the tails of the planes. Some were on fire. But at the end, Ghost Rider, the hero, was safe.

Miss Lane said each speaker gave a fine reading report.

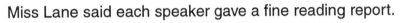

1. What happens each Friday in Miss Lane's class? _____

_____

2. What was Jay's book about? _____

_____

3. Tell what happened to the riders. _____

_____

_____

4. How many bike riders did not finish the race? _____

5. How would you feel about giving a speech to your class? _____

_____

PG#

1 *Circled words: sad, clap, hat, fad, said, clash, that, mad*
1) scratch 2) flag 3) grass 4) branch 5) slam 6) crack 7) glass 8) patch 9) band 10) wag

2 1) ax 2) tag 3) pan 4) hand 5) bag 6) rat 7) map 8) sack **Bottom)** *Sentences will vary.*

3 1) Circled words are *(left to right)*: land, tap, bath, lap, flash, crash, tramp 2) Checked words are *(left to right)*: stand, lamp, slap, last, stack, grab, lab 3) Underlined words are *(left to right)*: plan, gas, drag, brand, fact, grass, lamb, blast

4 Words that should be written inside the big 'A' are as follows *(in any order)*: flag, bath, rat, pat, pan, clash, stack, class, at, hat, clap, blast, quack, crash, cap, sack, mad, drag, last.

5 1) back 2) bag 3) bat 4) black 5) brass 6) class 7) flash 8) grab 9) grass 10) has 11) lamp 12) nap 13) pan 14) pants 15) pass 16) that

6 1) flat 2) tacks 3) lamp 4) lamb 5) bag 6) sand 7) grass 8) ranch 9) rag 10) glad 11) swam 12) last

7 1) stack 2) hatch 3) shack 4) stand 5) am 6) that 7) pants 8) land 9) lamp 10) cap 11) grab 12) lamb 13) back 14) act 15) grass 16) glass 17) fast 18) brand 19) cast 20) last

8 1) bath 2) pant 3) plant 4) class 5) sand 6) tramp 7) grant 8) path 9) ranch 10) lack 1) bath 2) class 3) grant 4) lack 5) pant 6) path 7) plant 8) ranch 9) sand 10) tramp

9 1) glad 2) past 3) brass 4) camp 5) rack 6) catch 7) ask 8) grant 9) gas 10) grab 11) and 12) slap 13) lack 14) bat 15) cast 16) class 1) and 2) ask 3) bat 4) brass 5) camp 6) cast 7) catch 8) class 9) gas 10) glad 11) grab 12) grant 13) lack 14) past 15) rack 16) slap

10

```
B A T O L S H D A N C E P Q D I D
R S A N D B A H S E E T H X N C P
B F O P H L T G A T H N K U S W L
L G R S Y A C C R A C K U V N L A
A O T O B E T N C L A S S R A P M
C I H O O L G C Q R Y W P Z P E B
K T H A N K B O H L M F A S T F G
A B C D E F Q H I J K L M N O D P
T A N Q R G A S S T H A T C A U A
V D W X Y Z S O O E A X I M G H S
M A T C H T K R R M N Q P A S Z T
S A T O G T U X E F L A G O Q R T
B P G L A S S F R A N C H H S A M
```

11 *Sentences will vary.*

12 1) pan 2) bag 3) last 4) jam 5) mad 6) fat 7) lamp 8) sack 9) lap 10) crab **Bottom)** *Answers will vary.*

13 1) sand 2) lamp 3) ax 4) band 5) rack 6) crash 7) bath 8) quack 9) gas 10) dam 1) ax 2) band 3) bath 4) crash 5) dam 6) gas 7) lamp 8) quack 9) rack 10) sand

14 1) bat 2) cash 3) grass 4) catch 5) back 6) pan 7) that 8) ask 9) black 10) bad 11) sad 12) sand **Bottom)** *Sentences will vary.*

15 1) tack 2) pants 3) grass 4) sack 5) rash 6) crack 7) black 8) patch 9) snap 10) brass

16 1) lawn 2) twig 3) sack 4) bum 5) break 6) happy 7) rest 8) boy 9) girl 10) pot 11) father 12) insect 13) money 14) ground 1) ant 2) bag 3) branch 4) cash 5) crack 6) dad 7) glad 8) grass 9) lad 10) land 11) lass 12) nap 13) pan 14) tramp

17 1) thin 2) subtract 3) good 4) first 5) front 6) slow 7) throw 8) sea 9) dry 10) tell 11) white 12) walked 13) happy 14) woman 1) add 2) ask 3) back 4) bad 5) black 6) catch 7) damp 8) fast 9) fat 10) land 11) last 12) man 13) ran 14) sad

18 1) grandstand 2) hatchback 3) backhand 4) handbag 5) hangman 6) sandman 7) handstand 8) crabgrass 9) backpack 1) back/pack 2) hand/stand 3) hand/bag 4) hatch/back 5) grand/stand 6) sand/man 7) back/hand 8) hang/man 9) crab/grass

19 1) Mack 2) He naps and snacks all day. 3) He heard a scratch near his mat. 4) a sack 5) no 6) The rat ran too fast.

20 1) a yak 2) Sam Slabb 3) teach Sally how to dance 4) He sang, clapped his hands, and tapped. 5) She ate it. 6) She was happy as a clam.

21 *Circled words: send, shell, neck, when, dress, sled, yell, tent, chest, west* 1) chest 2) dent 3) mend 4) spend 5) belt 6) rent 7) tent 8) nest 9) shell 10) wren

22 1) bell 2) egg 3) leg 4) nest 5) pet 6) shell 7) net 8) web **Bottom)** *Sentences will vary.*

23 **Top)** swept, beg, chest, vest, rent, pest, mend **Middle)** fled, bless, west, smell, sled, sell, then **Bottom)** jest, melt yell, sped, next, dress, when, wed

24 **Top)** Words that should be written inside the big 'E' are as follows *(in any order):* test, yes, felt, stretch, pet, bet, kept, hen, bend, belt, them, when, swept, press, next, lend, chest, egg **Bottom)** *Sentences will vary.*

25 1) slept 2) check 3) bled 4) shelf 5) test 6) egg 7) rent 8) shell 9) mend 10) spend

26 1) lend 2) slept 3) bed 4) met 5) keg 6) swept 7) pen 8) wed 9) men 10) chest 1) went 2) pet 3) desk 4) vest 5) less 6) kept 7) fell 8) chess 9) mess 10) test

27 1) cent 2) swell 3) spent 4) wren 5) belt 6) smell 7) help 8) shed 9) sled 10) fled 11) spell 12) trend 13) lend 14) rent 15) melt 16) neck 1) belt 2) cent

PG#

3) fled　4) help　5) lend　6) melt　7) neck　8) rent
9) shed　10) sled　11) smell　12) spell　13) spent
14) swell　15) trend　16) wren

28

```
V E N T L S W E S T C E P T N E C
S S A N D B O Y S E E T H A N C L
H F O P Q N E C K T N N K U S X E
E G R B Y Z T A Z E E C U V N L S
L D N E P S I N H D A D S R A X S
L I H S O L G W L R N W Y D N C L
N E X T N K B E C E M F A T E Y G
A B L E S S W H B J K S T R E S S
T A N Q R S K S S T H H T C H U E
V D W S T R E T C H L E N D G H N
M R T C H T P R R M N D T A S Z T
R E N T G T X A M N D M E L T R T
B D G L A T R E N D N C K E P T M
```

29　1-8) *Sentences will vary.*　1) bend　2) bled　3) fed　4) fled

30　**Top)** Matched together in any of the 7 circles, the word pairs are: chest/west, deck/check, sped/bled, spell/well, when/then, dent/spent, dress/press　**Bottom)** *Answers will vary.*

31　1) chest　2) pen　3) slept　4) pet　5) red　6) bell　7) tent
8) mess　9) well　10) test　**Bottom)** *Answers will vary.*

32　1) egg　2) hen　3) shed　4) chest　5) test　6) belt
7) neck　8) pen　9) bell　10) ten　1) bell　2) belt　3) chest
4) egg　5) hen　6) neck　7) pen　8) shed　9) ten　10) test

33　1) west　2) pen　3) red　4) hen　5) yes　6) tenth　7) bed
8) bent　9) them　10) best　11) men　12) leg　**Bottom)**
Sentences will vary.

34　1) married　2) placed　3) snoozed　4) jewel　5) iron
6) sniff　7) cot　8) exam　9) cried　10) shout　11) finish
12) damp　13) gown　14) fix　**Bottom)** *Sentences will vary.*

35　1) dry　2) more　3) women　4) came　5) worst　6) saved
7) woke　8) ask　9) buy　10) begin　11) freeze　12) no
13) whisper　14) rooster　1) best　2) end　3) hen　4) less
5) melt　6) men　7) sell　8) slept　9) spent　10) tell
11) went　12) wet　13) yell　14) yes

36　1) Betsy　2) old elm tree　3) three　4) a very bad storm
5) squirrels　6) having friends that would lend a hand
when trouble came

37　1) a sled　2) at Speck's Store　3) he went to Speck's
Store　4) $10.00　5) $7.00　6) He earned $2.00 helping
Mr. Bell and his uncle Ted sent him $1.00.

38　*Circled words: thick, chin, skin, twin, mint, will, print,
dish, swim*　1) trick　2) fish　3) milk　4) slid　5) ditch
6) wrist　7) chick　8) lid　9) hill　10) swim

39　1) fish　2) drill　3) ship　4) bricks　5) hill　6) chick
7) whip　8) lid　**Bottom)** *Sentences will vary.*

40　**Top)** kid, chick, drift, limb, stiff, lift, shin, wish
Middle) wrist, win, thin, quick, rich, tip, skip
Bottom) fish, grid, click, swim, slick, chill, skin

41　**Top)** Words that should be written inside the big 'I' are
as follows *(in any order):* bid, fit, lick, split, hid, trick,
pick, chin, fix, fish, drift, kick, gift, brick, ink, lick, limb,
hip, ditch.　**Bottom)** *Sentences will vary.*

42　1) ship　2) fill　3) dig　4) cliff　5) flip　6) silk　7) spill
8) trick　9) bill　10) limb　11) quilt　12) hit

43　1) nick　2) grit　3) knit　4) grip　5) whip　6) mink　7) pitch
8) skin　9) twin　10) cliff　11) witch　12) ditch　13) miss
14) print　15) quick　16) rich　17) spill　18) thin　19) trick
20) brick

44　1) slit　2) drill　3) quill　4) spilt　5) switch　6) drift　7) kid
8) risk　9) hid　10) thin　1) drift　2) drill　3) hid　4) kid
5) quill　6) risk　7) slit　8) spilt　9) switch　10) thin

45　1) pitch　2) wind　3) wrist　4) whip　5) limp　6) kiss
7) ink　8) gift　9) wish　10) still　11) cliff　12) spill　13) grid
14) skip　15) tint　16) chill　1) chill　2) cliff　3) gift
4) grid　5) ink　6) kiss　7) limp　8) pitch　9) skip　10) spill
11) still　12) tint　13) whip　14) wind　15) wish　16) wrist

46

```
B Z H I T F M G H J K L L I F T X
I Y Z U F I Z R T N S M O P Q R T
G S T U D V Z I D K K B C D E F I
G H J K L M S N O P I Q R S T U L
L L I F V W X Y Z X Y C D F P I L
H J T B D S M I X O I M I H M N Y
S Q S K I N X V S L I P Y A E E V
K A B C D E F G I H G K L M N O P
I S T U V W X I T Y I N Z X Y Z I
P A R I S K B C D E F G H J K L H
X W D L D W V K C I R B X Y Z D W
J I G L H E F T U F Z R S L M N D
B X Y Z B R Q D G E E T T I U Q A
```

47　1-8) *Sentences will vary.*　1) ship　2) silk　3) slip　4) spin

48　1) fish　2) quilt　3) wrist　4) dish　5) kid　6) limb　7) wind
8) chin　9) ship　10) pig　1) chin　2) dish　3) fish　4) kid
5) limb　6) pig　7) quilt　8) ship　9) wind　10) wrist

49　1) milk　2) big　3) kiss　4) sixth　5) swift　6) brick
7) pig　8) sick　9) skip　10) trick　11) silk　12) kick
Bottom) *Sentences will vary.*

50　1) choose　2) ill　3) smile　4) tear　5) cut　6) drop
7) wink　8) boat　9) sip　10) hole　11) stop　12) huge
13) mind　14) fast　**Bottom)** *Sentences will vary.*

PG#

51 1) fat 2) frown 3) stand 4) hers 5) bright 6) break 7) out 8) poor 9) lose 10) slow 11) didn't 12) start 13) will 14) won't 1) did 2) dim 3) fix 4) grin 5) his 6) in 7) quick 8) quit 9) rich 10) sick 11) sit 12) thin 13) will 14) win

52 1) Silver River 2) very still 3) there was a thick mist 4) tall cliffs 5) The mist thinned and the moon shone through. 6) no

53 1) Dixon City 2) Winterdale 3) 15 4) football 5) 6 to 6 6) 13 to 6 7) the Wimps

54 *Circled words: pond, soap, lost, hop, frost, off, drop, not, boss, pot, block* 1) long 2) cross 3) pond 4) cloth 5) frog 6) knot 7) flock 8) lost 9) stop 10) rob

55 1) clock 2) rock 3) box 4) sock 5) cot 6) lock 7) mop 8) fox **Bottom)** *Sentences will vary.*

56 **Top)** flop, stop, spot, shop, lot, shot, snob, log **Middle)** smog, lock, jot, bond, block, fog, frog, hop **Bottom)** lot, plot, fond, hot, cost, blot

57 **Top)** Words that should be written inside the big 'O' are as follows *(in any order)*: doll, pop, cloth, log, fond, pond, lot, frog, rob, top, cross, smog, frost, rod, blond, hot, stock, dog, knot. **Bottom)** *Sentences will vary.*

58 1) sock 2) mop 3) drop 4) frost 5) frog 6) cloth 7) flock 8) knot 9) knock 10) job 11) pot 12) cot **Bottom)** *Sentences will vary.*

59 1) rock 2) mop 3) crop 4) odd 5) lock 6) flock 7) sock 8) blond 9) knot 10) block 11) smog 12) shot 13) got 14) stop 15) frost 16) stock 17) toss 18) pond 19) not 20) drop

60 1) blot 2) lock 3) frog 4) log 5) off 6) pond 7) boss 8) shop 9) clock 10) sock 1) blot 2) boss 3) clock 4) frog 5) lock 6) log 7) off 8) pond 9) sock 10) shop

61 1) rock 2) pond 3) flock 4) stock 5) blot 6) chop 7) spot 8) frost 9) lost 10) cross 11) smog 12) job 13) clock 14) box 15) bond 16) cloth 1) blot 2) bond 3) box 4) chop 5) clock 6) cloth 7) cross 8) flock 9) frost 10) job 11) lost 12) pond 13) rock 14) smog 15) spot 16) stock

62

```
K A F L O C K D A H O P P Q D T F
N S M N D B M T O S S T R J N R R
O D D P Q L J G A T H L O S T V O
T G R S Y Z T T O P E C D V N Z S
A H T A B E D N O L B S G R A M T
S I H O O L G I Q R X W E Z P E B
O T C R O S S O B L M F A S T F G
F B C D E F G H L J K L F T V P P
T A N Q K C O L O Z H L Y O H U K
V D W T Y Z F O C M A O I C G H C
M A O C H T F R K N N T K S Z O
X L Y O G T U X E R L A G O Q R R
B O S S A C L O T H N C H H S A M
```

PG#

63 **Top)** *Sentences will vary.* 1) block 2) blot 3) soft 4) stock

64 1) cot 2) cost 3) pot 4) smog 5) soft 6) jog 7) box 8) dock 9) top 10) log **Bottom)** *Answers will vary.*

65 **Top)** Matched together in any of the 6 circles, the word pairs are: chop/shop, block/shock, hot/cot, cross/moss, rod/pod, lost/frost **Bottom)** *Answers will vary.*

66 1) smog 2) frost 3) frog 4) hog 5) doll 6) dog 7) pot 8) knot 9) ox 10) sock **Bottom)** *Sentences will vary.*

67 1) *flock* 2) rock 3) mop 4) clock 5) soft 6) shock 7) toss 8) job 9) dog 10) pot

68 1) soft 2) frog 3) blond 4) off 5) pot 6) fox 7) top 8) mop 9) box 10) sock 11) tock 12) chop **Bottom)** *Sentences will vary.*

69 1) rap 2) spoil 3) stone 4) lid 5) store 6) throw 7) bed 8) leap 9) cut 10) quit 11) dad 12) policeman 13) pan 14) child 1) chop 2) cop 3) cot 4) hop 5) knock 6) pop 7) pot 8) rock 9) rot 10) shop 11) stop 12) top 13) toss 14) tot

70 1) even 2) found 3) on 4) hard 5) off 6) laugh 7) go 8) cold 9) catch 10) bottom 1) hot 2) lost 3) odd 4) off 5) on 6) sob 7) soft 8) stop 9) top 10) toss

71 1) frog legs 2) to the pond 3) foggy 4) on a big rock in the middle of the pond 5) hearing the frog speak 6) It hopped away.

72 1) Boppo 2) Farmer Todd 3) It was too high. 4) a log 5) They ran after him. 6) He ran to his den and never trotted near Farmer Todd's chicken yard again.

73 *Circled words: mud, stub, fun, plum, lunch, nut, tub, slum, stuck* 1) shrub 2) plug 3) sunk 4) brush 5) bunk 6) dust 7) lunch 8) mush 9) plum 10) truck

74 1) drum 2) sun 3) jug 4) plum 5) brush 6) truck 7) hut 8) tub **Bottom)** *Sentences will vary.*

75 **Top)** bug, drug, brush, bluff, bump, crust, gun **Middle)** plum, much, stung, plug, crumb, rust, such, stuff, crust **Bottom)** us, tuck, thump, sun, bud, dull, dug, duck

76 **Top)** Words that should be written inside the big 'U' are as follows *(in any order)*: plug, club, rug, plum, chum, dug, punt, shrub, grub, rut, cub, luck, sun, spun, blunt, drum, strum, thump, dump. **Bottom)** *Sentences will vary.*

77 1) shut 2) fun 3) plum 4) chum 5) rush 6) chump 7) dust 8) much 9) muff 10) crumb 11) hung 12) such 13) tuck 14) us 15) crush 16) up 17) junk 18) rug 19) lunch 20) mud

78 1) lump 2) thump 3) sum 4) bump 5) crust 6) dust 7) hunt 8) dull 9) mug 10) must 1) bump 3) crust 4) dull 5) dust 6) hunt 7) mug 8) must 9) sum 10) thump

PG#

79 1) bunch 2) sprung 3) grunt 4) blush 5) strut 6) scrub 7) hunch 8) lunch 9) spun 10) stump 11) plug 12) stub 13) cluck 14) club 15) trust 16) nut 1) blush 2) bunch 3) club 4) cluck 5) grunt 6) hunch 7) lunch 8) nut 9) plug 10) scrub 11) sprung 12) spun 13) strut 14) stub 15) stump 16) trust

80

```
R U S H L L U M P N C E R Q S
R S K N D B O Y S E E H U S H
H F U R H S U R B T H N N U U
U G L S Y Z T A Z P E C U V T
G H L U C K I N U L A S S R F
C I H O O F G I Q R B U T Z U
H U T A F K B O B L M F A S S
U B C U E F G M U L P L M N S
S A P Q R G A S G T H M F C H
K D W R B N S O O S T U C K G
M A T C H T K R R M N D T A S
C L U M P T U S U C H K C U D
```

81 **Top)** *Sentences will vary.* 1) buck 2) bug 3) dump 4) dust

82 **Top)** Matched together in any of the 7 circles, the word pairs are: scrub/club, plug/smug, thump/plump, stunt/punt, drum/chum, truck/stuck, flush/blush **Bottom)** *Answers will vary.*

83 1) tub 2) hung 3) crust 4) dug 5) brush 6) hunt 7) bump 8) sun 9) dust 10) bus

84 1) run 2) lunch 3) gum 4) thumb 5) brush 6) duck 7) plum 8) hum 9) shrub 10) sun 11) hug 12) bus **Bottom)** *Sentences will vary.*

85 1) insect 2) bed 3) dirt 4) bottle 5) close 6) pull 7) leap 8) hit 9) dollar 10) cup 11) cozy 12) friend 13) fat 14) eat 1) buck 2) bug 3) bunk 4) chum 5) dust 6) jug 7) jump 8) mug 9) munch 10) plump 11) punch 12) shut 13) snug 14) tug

86 1) tub 2) nut 3) trunk 4) truck 5) rug 6) skunk 7) gun 8) drum 9) mud 10) bus 11) bump 12) dust **Bottom)** *Sentences will vary.*

87 1) truck driver 2) nuts 3) to the Crunchy Candy Factory 4) He heard a funny clunk under the hood. 5) men in a bus

88 1) Bucky and Buddy 2) Thumbs Up 3) an old trunk 4) to store secret stuff 5) Chuck

89 *Circled words: them, thin, fled, stop, win, glass, tub, best, flat, club* 1) miss 2) strap 3) dish 4) lamp 5) stuck 6) hatch 7) lamb 8) shelf 9) stiff 10) sack

PG#

90 **Top)** flop, step, flat, stub, split, flub, shin, plot **Middle)** rag, clock, stab, bench, pin, tag, bust **Bottom)** best, fin, tub, glad, top, black, test, shop

91 **Short A)** stack, cap, rat, flag, flap **Short E)** best, sped, spend, bled, check. **Short I)** slid, skin, brick, thin skip **Short O)** shop, block, drop, mop, chop **Short U)** much, hunt, tub, stub, rub

92 1) stuck 2) miss 3) chop 4) lamp 5) chimp 6) fin 7) rag 8) bed 9) chick 10) lamb 11) bit 12) tan 1) bed 2) bit 3) chick 4) chimp 5) chop 6) fin 7) lamb 8) lamp 9) miss 10) rag 11) stuck 12) tan

93 1) patch 2) chest 3) chop 4) trim 5) trunk 6) cliff 7) glass 8) duck 9) spot 10) spell 11) egg 12) knot 13) quilt 14) club 15) glad 16) smell 17) bunch 18) twin 19) sock 10) bell

94 1) grass 2) shed 3) shop 4) dish 5) sun 6) cash 7) fell 8) pin **Bottom)** *Answers will vary.*

95 1) s-n 2) s-h 3) g-r 4) s-h 5) c-h 6) t-r 7) c-l 8) b-r 1) chum 2) grin 3) clock 4) ship 5) shell 6) truck 7) branch 8) snack

96 **Top)** Words that should be circled are: ham, tip, hop, rag, rut, hid, hen, rob, pin, nut, mad, pot, red, bun, bell **Short A)** ham, rag, mad **Short E)** hen, red, bell **Short I)** tip, hid, pin **Short O)** hop, rob, pot **Short U)** rut, nut, bun **Bottom)** *Sentences will vary.*

97 1) *branch* 2) cab 3) fresh 4) shed 5) odd 6) silk 7) dust 8) rust 9) hatch 10) spend

98 **Top)** Lines should be drawn connecting the following pairs: bath--tub, back--stop, egg--plant, dish--cloth, drum--stick, egg--nog, hand--cuff, hill--top **Bottom)** *Sentences will vary.*

99 **Top)** Lines should be drawn connecting the following pairs: cat--fish, egg--shell, dust--pan, gun--man, pick--up, back--hand, hand--gun, up--set **Bottom)** *Sentences will vary.*

100 1) drumstick 2) pickup 3) dishcloth 4) catfish 5) upset 6) gunmen 7) eggshell 8) bathtub 1) dish/cloth 2) gun/men 3) pick/up 4) bath/tub 5) up/set 6) egg/shell 7) drum/stick 8) cat/fish **Bottom)** *Sentences will vary.*

101 1) *Stories will vary*

102 1) Frogs live in ponds. 2) They dig a hole in the mud at the bottom of the pond. 3) They come back to the top when the days get warm 4) Frogs lay their eggs near the top of the water. 5) At first, a baby frog is much like a fish. 6) Frogs stay near water to keep their skin wet.

103 1) in a truck 2) unpack the truck 3) Jack 4) six 5) a skunk 6) He had a swell dad who took him camping.

104 1) Billy 2) eight 3) Cal Crab and Sam Clam 4) He shuts his shell. 5) Billy 6) when they see a big shark fin

105 *Circled words:* coax, prize, chain, steam, throat, stay, leave, cute, shine, float, throw, wheeze, phone. **1)** braid **2)** pine **3)** foam **4)** toad **5)** mule **6)** hate **7)** cream **8)** time **9)** fumes

106 **1)** tray **2)** plate **3)** maid **4)** lake **5)** crate **6)** cane **7)** hay **8)** chain **Bottom)** *Sentences will vary.*

107 **1)** cage **2)** paint **3)** grade **4)** mail **5)** shade **6)** jade **7)** face **8)** paid **9)** cape **10)** blame **11)** bake **12)** skate **1)** bake **2)** blame **3)** cage **4)** cape **5)** face **6)** grade **7)** jade **8)** mail **9)** paid **10)** paint **11)** shade **12)** skate

108 **1)** beet **2)** seal **3)** feet **4)** beak **5)** wheel **6)** peach **7)** heel **8)** leaf

109 **1)** leap **2)** beat **3)** seal **4)** steam **5)** stream **6)** meet **7)** steep **8)** seed **9)** sheet **10)** meat **11)** mean **12)** breeze **Bottom)** *Sentences will vary.*

110 **1)** tie **2)** file **3)** pie **4)** slide **5)** dime **6)** tire **7)** kite **8)** lime **Bottom)** *Sentences will vary.*

111 **1)** five **2)** size **3)** mile **4)** write **5)** dime **6)** hike **7)** price **8)** white **9)** wipe **10)** ride **11)** tie **12)** pile **1~8)** *Answers will vary.*

112 **1)** boat **2)** hoe **3)** goat **4)** coat **5)** bow **6)** toast **7)** loaf **8)** doe

113 **1)** oats **2)** toe **3)** show **4)** doe **5)** goat **6)** low **7)** toast **8)** grow **9)** road **10)** row **11)** float **12)** bow **Bottom)** *Sentences will vary.*

114 **1)** rose **2)** fuse **3)** cone **4)** mule **5)** cube **6)** bone **7)** nose **8)** phone **Bottom)** *Sentences will vary.*

115 **1)** toad **2)** nose **3)** live **4)** sail **5)** mule **6)** bleed **7)** pray **8)** slide **Bottom)** *Sentences will vary.*

116 **Top)** The words that should be circled are: row, beat, fine, play, hide, cream, sail, soap, throat, chain, line, please, save, seed, kite, bone. **Long A)** play, sail, chain, save **Long E)** beat, cream, please, seed **Long I)** fine, hide, line, kite **Long O)** row, soap, throat, bone **Bottom)** *Sentences will vary.*

117 **Top)** mule, screen, pray, braid, tow, meal, tie, toast **Middle)** coat, streak, stay, maid, mile, made, feast **Bottom)** chain, file, toe, roast, bake, cream, fume, blow

118 **1)** meet **2)** meat **3)** meet **1)** heel **2)** heel **3)** heal **1)** week **2)** weak **3)** week **1)** pail **2)** pale **3)** pail **1)** rode **2)** rode **3)** road **1)** maid **2)** made **3)** made

119 **1)** croak **2)** crime **3)** beef **4)** seam **5)** these **6)** brain **7)** gain **8)** close **9)** mow **10)** slate **11)** while **12)** cute **13)** own **14)** pie **15)** sweep **16)** reef **1)** beef **2)** brain **3)** close **4)** crime **5)** croak **6)** cute **7)** gain **8)** mow **9)** own **10)** pie **11)** reef **12)** seam **13)** slate **14)** sweep **15)** these **16)** while

120

```
R F S G H D W O R C N I K F S G R L
B D T Y L M H K A B R C L V H K D E
A B R C D E I F G H I A J K L M N U
O P A Q R S L T U V E W X Y Z E O F
S H I N E J E I B R O A M D C A X I
P R N O T U V W I Z F R D V O P Q R
O L J R V I B D O W X A B Y A R T D
K T V U A L E A V E S N M A L E I F
E S R V X A L M N E O P Q R M S T U
Q P L T E I X B C K T O N A I F D V
R O I I B A N Q D F G H R I J A B W
K L M E N O A B E D S F U M E Z Y X
```

121 **1)** heel **2)** rose **3)** pine **4)** green **5)** vine **6)** cone **7)** write **8)** eel **9)** leaves **10)** smoke **Bottom)** *Sentences will vary.*

122 **1)** His fine garden and beautiful yard. **2)** weeding, mowing, hoeing, spading and sowing seeds **3)** sweet peas **4)** beans, tomatoes **5)** The snails feast on his plants.

123 **1)** The students speak about books they have been reading. **2)** a five-mile bike race **3)** One rider ran over a nail, one broke the wheel, one lost his chain, and only five racers crossed the finish line. **4)** four **5)** *Answers will vary*

Other books available from . . .

◆◆◆◆ REMEDIA PUBLICATIONS ◆◆◆◆

Essential Vocabulary—*Grades 4–12/Rdg. Level 3–4*
Supermarket Words .... Item Number REM 931A
Restaurant Words .... Item Number REM 931B
Department Store Words .... Item Number REM 931C
Computer Words .... Item Number REM 979A
Survival Words .... Item Number REM 910

Life Skills
Reading—*Grades 4–12/Rdg. Level 3–4*
The Newspaper .... Item Number REM 417
Labels & Packages .... Item Number REM 430
Ads & Coupons .... Item Number REM 431
Directories & Guides .... Item Number REM 432
Catalogs .... Item Number REM 433
Filling Out Forms .... Item Number REM 435

* Vocabulary—*Grades 7–12/Rdg. Level 4–5*
Consumer Words .... Item Number REM 930A
Work Place Words .... Item Number REM 930B
Independent Living Words .... Item Number REM 930D
Personal Care Words .... Item Number REM 930E

* Math—*Rdg. Level 3–4*
Math in the Mall .... *Grades 4–12* .... Item Number REM 598A
Math at Home .... *Grades 4–12* .... Item Number REM 598B
Best Buys .... *Grades 4–12* .... Item Number REM 598D
Money Sense .... *Grades 4–12* .... Item Number REM 598E
Checkbook Math .... *Grades 4–6* .... Item Number REM 524

Comprehension—*Grades 4–8/Rdg. Level 3–4*
In the Kitchen .... Item Number REM 454A
Understanding Instructions .... Item Number REM 454D

High-Interest Reading
* Comprehension—*Grades 4–8*
Comprehension Quickies ...... Rdg. Level 2 .... Item Number REM 440
Comprehension Quickies ...... Rdg. Level 3 .... Item Number REM 441

Critical Thinking—*Grades 4–6/Rdg. Level 3–4*
Making Decisions .... Item Number REM 204B

* Comprehension & Research Skills—*Grades 4–12/Rdg. Level 3–4*
Presidents .... Item Number REM 418
Inventors .... Item Number REM 419
Strange Tales .... Item Number REM 437

Understanding—*Grades 4–8/Rdg. Level 3–4*
Natural Phenomena .... Item Number REM 453
Reading to Understand .... Item Number REM 445

* Cloze Procedure—*Grades 4–8*
Context Clues .... Rdg. Level 2 .... Item Number REM 412
Context Clues .... Rdg. Level 3 .... Item Number REM 413

*More titles in this series are available.

. . . and much more!

NOTES